GOOD MORNING, SUNDAY

*108 reflections
for meditation*

VEENA CHATANI

with illustrations by Susan Clare

R^ethink

First published in Great Britain in 2023
by Rethink Press (www.rethinkpress.com)

© Copyright Veena Chatani

Cover painting and illustrations by Susan Clare

*"Feeling gratitude and not expressing it
is like wrapping a present and not giving it."*

—William Arthur Ward

In gratitude to my children, Praveen and Minali.
This one's for you.

To my parents,

When we are born, our parents are our world;
then the world lures us away like the Pied Piper.
This morning, I choose to show gratitude to
you for the values you instilled in me, for your
unconditional love and support throughout my
life, and for a simple and wholesome childhood.

I remember your goodness, kindness, and
generosity. Though you are no longer with me,
I can still feel your love running through
my being.

I love you,
V

Contents

Introduction   *1*

1 Sunday Morning   3
2 The Truth   4
3 Finding Balance   9
4 Gratitude   11
5 The Power Of Attention   12
6 Painting   13
7 Harmony   15
8 A Smile   17
9 The Mind   18
10 Taste   21
11 Encouragement   23
12 Connected To Body, Breath, Mind   25
13 Tradition   27
14 What Will People Think?   29
15 The Ocean   32
16 Stillness   33
17 The River   35
18 Light   39
19 The Beach   40
20 Minimum Daily Requirement   41
21 Healing Power Of Sound   43
22 Listening   45
23 Above All The Noise   47
24 The Road Less Traveled   49

25	The Mountains	50
26	Letting Go	52
27	Intuition	54
28	Sharing	55
29	Home	56
30	The Attic	58
31	The Daily Practice	61
32	The Plunge	63
33	Patterns	65
34	Exploring The Light	67
35	Passion	70
36	My Dog	72
37	The Orchid	75
38	Nature	77
39	Fallen Leaves	78
40	Surrendering Control	80
41	The Breath	82
42	Solar Panels	85
43	Beauty	87
44	Sound	88
45	Me	89
46	Injuries	91
47	Nature's Little Miracles	93
48	Goodbye	96
49	Aging	97
50	Nature Walks	99
51	That Gut Feeling	102
52	Nourishment	104
53	The Pause Button	106
54	The Observer	107

55	Birthdays	110
56	The Anchor	111
57	Journaling	114
58	Self-discipline	116
59	Surrender	118
60	Being Present	121
61	Signs From The Universe	123
62	To Serve	125
63	Humility	126
64	The Spirit Of Wonder	127
65	Commitment	129
66	Stay Awhile	131
67	A Little Bit Of Nutmeg	133
68	Feeling Grounded	135
69	Silver Linings	138
70	The Sound Of Silence	140
71	Dancing	143
72	Planting Seeds	144
73	Trust	147
74	The Silence Within	149
75	The Breeze	151
76	Detachment	152
77	Measure	154
78	Encouragement	156
79	Forgiveness	157
80	A Walk On The Hill	160
81	The Space Within	162
82	Strength	164
83	Seeing	165
84	Motivation	167

85 Savasana 169
86 Motherhood 171
87 Recharging 173
88 The Little Girl 175
89 Words 178
90 A Lump Of Clay 180
91 Experience 183
92 Intend And Allow 185
93 Music 187
94 The Journey 189
95 Choice 190
96 The Places I Call Home 192
97 Silence 194
98 Coffee Breaks 196
99 The Present Moment 199
100 Simplicity 201
101 All One 203
102 Letters 204
103 Commitment To A Gratitude Practice 207
104 Birds 209
105 The Guest Room 211
106 Sparkle 213
107 The Backstage Crew 214
108 108 Drops 217

Building A Practice 219
Acknowledgments 221
The Author 223

Introduction

December 1, 2018

It's December 1, and I've been up since 4 a.m.

My to-do list is running through my head like a marathon runner. If this were a race, I would surely win. "'Tis the season to be jolly," they say. Then why am I feeling so overwhelmed?

Instead of thinking about the lists, the work, and the "partridge in the pear tree," I decide that I will shift my mindset, and think about the things I am grateful for.

That is how my practice began.

It was powerful.

My writing freed me from the weight of daily duties and enabled me to stay calm and grounded. Over time it evolved into reflections shared on Sunday mornings before my meditation practice.

This book is a collection of 108 of my favorite reflections.[*]

I hope they spark inspiration for personal growth through your practice of gratitude and awaken a curiosity for meditation. There is no real beginning or end; simply open to a random page and allow the words to settle in.

---

[*] The number 108 is an auspicious number in many eastern and yogic traditions. Mala beads are a strand of 108 beads that are often used in mantra or japa meditation. The beads serve as a physical anchor to remind us to return to the present moment.

1

Sunday Morning

Sunday mornings
when there is
nowhere to go,
nothing to do,
no agenda,
no wake-up calls,
no immediate plans,
nothing pressing on the to-do list...
just a morning to be.
To wake up when my eyes open.
Somehow, it's quieter than any other morning.
It sounds like even the birds take it easy,
easy like a Sunday morning.

Good morning, Sunday.
Let's meditate.

2

The Truth

As I sit on my patio, I look out onto the
lagoon. This morning the water is still.
It looks like a pane of polished glass. I see
the reflection of the land across the bay in
the water. The houses cast an elongated
white image, as if they are trying to stretch
themselves a few stories higher—reaching,
high on their tippy toes.

As my gaze moves in closer, I notice the
reflection of the dock and the four sun-
bleached wooden Adirondack chairs in the
water. Their reflection is the exact image
of the actual chairs that sit on the dock.
The water is motionless, the reflections
so precise that if I could turn my vision
upside down, I would think that I was
looking at the physical chairs. The blue sky
is clear and flawless. Another hot summer
day is expected when the wind is possible.

Suddenly a boat passes by, creating some movement in the water. I see soft ripples slowly growing into larger waves, causing the reflection to change; I see dancing chairs. But the chairs are not dancing. They are still in the same place on the dock, sitting peacefully as before.

Their reflection has changed.

My perception has changed.

The chairs have remained the same.

As the day continues, the wind picks up, and the waves get choppier. The reflection that was there this morning has disappeared.

It is gone with the wind.

Is my vision impaired?

I look at the dock: The chairs are still there, exactly where I saw them.

They have not moved. The wind has not
disturbed them.

They are steadfast and grounded, solid as
trees rooted in the earth.

This is the truth.

The truth remains the same; it never
changes.

What changes is our perception.

What changes is our mind, disturbed by
the slightest movement.

How can I continue to see the truth?

Stop looking down at the reflection that is
not the reality.

Stop looking up at the sky, waiting for the
wind to blow you the answer.

Choose to look straight ahead at the present moment,

where the truth sits right in front of you, unchanging,

like the Adirondack chair waiting for you to take a seat.

Good morning, Sunday.
Let's meditate.

3

Finding Balance

On my walk around Lake Naomi yesterday,
I noticed a collection of stones, carefully
stacked and balanced, waiting to see if
something would disrupt its equilibrium.
Would it be rain, the wind, or a human?
I was tempted to place a few more stones on
top to continue nature's game of Jenga, my
curiosity daring me to take the challenge.
I decided to pause and take a picture instead,
as it reminded me of how often we do this to
ourselves. We pile up our days with so many
responsibilities, and take on burdens, until
one day something throws us off.

Finding the right balance is essential if we
want to find stability in life. This differs for
each individual, and changes throughout
our lifetime. Some days we can take on
more than others. When we play Jenga, we
take a moment to pause and examine the
options and possibilities, before we make

our next strategic move. We seldom do this in our own lives. Are we balancing our time for work, play, and rest appropriately? Or are we piling on too many rocks, so that one day we may topple over when the weather gets stormy? If we are resting too much, we could lose our flexibility. Can we move around some of the rocks without disturbing the harmony?

Let's take a moment to contemplate this equation in our lives, and play a little Jenga.

Good morning, Sunday.
Let's meditate.

4

Gratitude

We use the words "thank you" all the time. We were taught when we were children that this is the polite response when receiving something. However, gratitude is so much more than just saying thank you. When someone looks at you with gratitude, you can feel it radiating as you look into their eyes.

Gratitude is in your bones, in the core of your being; it's what your mom meant when she said, "Say thank you like you mean it." I put up a gratitude tree in my store to share my experience and asked customers and staff to fill it with their messages. Some wrote with ease, and others gave me a strange look and couldn't understand the purpose or concept. Gratitude can't be taught; it can only be felt. I am grateful for being able to connect with the gratitude that lives inside of me.

Good morning, Sunday.
Let's meditate.

5

The Power Of Attention

Where attention goes, energy flows.

When we commit ourselves with one-pointed attention, anything is possible. Whether it's riding a bike, learning another language, starting a new career, meditating, or even sticking with a twenty-five-day gratitude practice, it can be done. It may not always turn out the way you expect it to, but as long as you stick with it, the power is all yours, and you are sure to feel the benefits of commitment.

A friend of mine ends her emails to me with the words "more power." I have never quite understood what she means. At first, it reminded me of how superheroes might greet each other, and I imagined them striking a pose. However, now that I think about it, the more power of attention we have, the more successful we will be in achieving our goal.

Good morning, Sunday.
Let's meditate.

6

Painting

When I went to my first painting class, I looked at my palette of red, yellow, blue, a touch of black and white. "That's it? What about the other colors?" I asked. My teacher looked at me and said: "You are the artist. Create them."

We create the other colors on our palettes by mixing and experimenting. Thus every artist's piece looks different, even though they may be painting the same scene. Formerly, even the paint had to be created from nature, and canvases were made by hand. Now we go to the store, buy some brushes, choose from an array of colors, grab a canvas, and we are all set.

Starting with only three colors forces us to use our creative instincts to discover. We take our time to contemplate while carefully selecting the perfect combination of blue and red to make our purple, or yellow and blue to make our green. This sense of mindfulness slows us down and allows us to connect with our inner being. It's almost like preparing for meditation. Depending on our mood that day, our blue may be brighter, our red may be deeper. Once we have created our color, our brushstrokes tell our story. How we paint reflects the quality of our mind and brings our emotions to light on the canvas, which adds significance to our painting.

Make your own orange, your own green, your own purple. Everyone's palette differs, depending on how they view their world, their life at that particular moment when the brush meets the canvas. In our modern days of instant gratification, we have gotten accustomed to immediate results. We have lost sight of the work that goes into making things. We have forgotten the little details, the foundation of greater appreciation.

What colors are you creating on your palette today? How are you painting your world? Are you thoughtfully selecting precisely the right color?

Good morning, Sunday.
Let's meditate.

7

Harmony

Last Tuesday, I sat at my piano. It had been a
long time since my fingers traveled across the
keys. I looked through a pile of my old piano
books. The pages looked torn, tired, and weary—
some yellowing, others missing. I chose one
that included some of my favorite pieces.
At first, I struggled. Each time I hit the wrong
key, I cringed at the noise it created. Three hours
later, I heard some improvement. Time became
insignificant as I drifted into a world of harmony
and entered a state of flow.

When two or more individual notes are played
together and form a cohesive whole, they are
in harmony, and we can hear that they belong
together. The notes are in agreement, and the
music is beautiful. When notes are in a chord,
they are in accord, and thus we can hear the
harmony. I know when I hit an incorrect key.
Sometimes this is obvious to everyone who is

listening. On other occasions, it is only noticeable to me, as I can feel that something is off.

We all have our harmony. When what we say, think, and do agree with each other, we live in harmony and create music. When they do not, we create noise. Sometimes the noise is on the outside, and everyone can hear it. Other times the noise is on the inside, and only we can feel it. One note can make a difference. When we are in tune, life flows like Beethoven's "Für Elise." Whether we are in A-minor or A-major event in life, there will be harmony when we play our scales right.

Good morning, Sunday.
Let's meditate.

8

A Smile

There is so much power in a smile. When we see
babies, we try to make them smile. This evokes
a warm feeling within us, a feeling of happiness,
contentment, and gratitude. There are "real" smiles
and "forced" smiles. When we smile genuinely, it
comes from within. You can see it in our eyes, as if
our soul is smiling. This is why the smile of a baby is
so powerful. Babies have no judgment; they are just
pure and in touch with their true essence. They have
nothing to hide, so when they smile it comes from
the heart.

When we smile, we have a positive impact on the
world around us and we invite feelings of happiness
into our lives. Today, when you sit in meditation,
without changing the expression on your face, think
about a smile. Think about the feeling behind a smile.
See how this lifts your heart. If the thought of a smile
can have this power, imagine what a real smile can do.

Good morning, Sunday.
Let's meditate.

9

The Mind

I received a purple bracelet last week as a token of
Alzheimer's Awareness Month. It was a reminder to
me of how precious our mind is.

We are more likely to take care of things that we can
see or touch. Our face, our body, our possessions.
It is the things we cannot see that we often ignore.
The mind is invisible but it is responsible for all our
thoughts and actions. It deserves our recognition, our
attention, and our care.

How do we attend to the mind? Even when we do take
care of our mind, there is still no guarantee that it will
serve us forever. Similar to a car, or a pair of shoes,
wear and tear is unavoidable. Aging is a guarantee,
and diseases are not always in our control, as some are
genetic and others are still mysteries being analyzed.
However, we can take the time to understand mental
health, to care for and nurture the mind, the same
way we would anything else we hold dear.

When investigating a new computer system for my business last week, I realized how similarly a computer and the human mind work. First of all, if we don't switch on the computer, it can't work. So turn it on, and get it moving. The salesperson pointed out that whether the system works the way it is supposed to depends highly on what we put into the system: "Garbage in is garbage out." If we feed our mind with violence, negativity, fear, greed, and gossip, we cannot expect compassion, positivity, calmness, generosity, and peace of mind.

Feeding the computer new data will give us more reports and keep it up to date. We can keep our mind sharp by learning new things, keeping it active, and eating healthily. Finally, resting the mind is essential if we want it to serve us for the rest of our existence. There is a lot of data stored in our mind; it takes time to shut down. On some days this may take longer than others, depending on how many programs were used. We begin by quitting, letting go of one program at a time, until finally, there is just one: the breath, the mantra, or the present moment. We allow our mind to rest in one thing, which can support and carry us into stillness. We choose one that is compatible, so we can shut down and rest the mind. In the morning, we will start where we left off.

Good morning, Sunday.
Let's meditate.

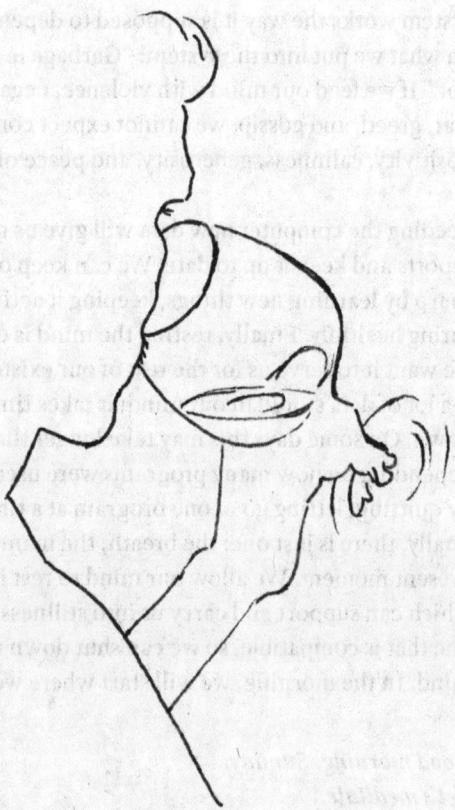

10

Taste

Eating and drinking are necessities for survival; tasting is optional. Once I take the first bite of my meal and determine whether it is satisfactory or requires salt, pepper, or hot sauce, the next few bites are not always as thoughtful. I may, at times, rush through my lunch at work. Other times I could become so engrossed in a dinner conversation that I lose touch with what is on my plate.

A few weeks ago, my husband, children, and I visited Napa, where we experienced the art of wine tasting. The sommelier asked us to swirl the wine around in the glass, releasing its aroma. We captured its bouquet and took a mindful sip, allowing the wine to settle in our mouths as parts of the tongue discovered the different flavors. This practice of attention was intriguing as it forced me to take my time to focus on precisely what I was tasting, one sip at a time.

The sommelier talked about the elements in the earth and the weather conditions while growing the grapes. In each sip, I could experience the careful preparation of the soil, the farmer planting the vines, and the grapes being picked at just the right time, crushed, blended, and stored with precision and accuracy to obtain the desired flavor. Could I taste the oak barrel that kept the wine? Or the oregano that was growing next to the vine?

When I consume my food mindfully and savor every bite, I notice that I don't require as much in quantity, as I enjoy and appreciate the quality and my palate is content. You can practice attention to taste with everything you consume, from the pine nut in your salad to the icing on your cake. Next time, instead of devouring your Swiss chocolate, take a small bite, appreciating and enjoying every nibble. A box of thirty pieces may last you one whole month.

Good morning, Sunday.
Let's meditate.

11

Encouragement

Encouragement is the act of giving someone support, confidence, or hope. Encouragement provides us with the strength and enthusiasm to accomplish the things that we are capable of doing. It is that extra push that gets us going: "the wind beneath our wings." Parents get so excited when their baby takes their first step. They smile, applaud, give reassuring comments, and help the child build confidence in their ability.

As we age, the necessity for encouragement never diminishes. We still need that extra support or pat on the back that helps us continue, even if it comes from ourselves. Some people thrive on awards or public recognition. Those who are modest cherish a smile or an uplifting comment.

Whatever the style of reassurance is, we must remember that what food is for the body, encouragement is for the mind. Be mindful that encouragement could cause us to feel arrogant or boastful once we achieve our goal. However, when we accept encouragement with humility as an innocent child does, it nurtures us into becoming a confident version of ourselves as we mature. Each step we take, from the first to the last, is more inspiring when we have cheerleaders by our side. There's nothing like a little "rah-rah" to lift our spirits.

Good morning, Sunday.
Let's meditate.

12

Connected To Body, Breath, Mind

It's 5:45 a.m. and −8 degrees Celsius—chilly for an island girl. I stand inside the main building, contemplating as I peek through the glass door at the Sri Vidya Shrine, a brand-new space for meditation built on the grounds of the Himalayan Institute, in Honesdale, Pennsylvania. It stands there glowing in the dark, looking serene and inviting. I will have to take the plunge and walk across the lawn, as the former meditation room, which is a convenient ten-second indoor walk from my room, is no longer open.

I suppose part of the practice is to welcome change and not get too attached to the past. I gather up my courage along with my long T-shirt, sweater, cashmere hoodie, overcoat, gloves, wool sox, boots, and shawl, and dash through the parking lot. According to The Weather Channel, it "feels like" −12 degrees Celsius. I am frozen, I can't feel anything, so I wouldn't know. I quickly walk through the large front door, take off my shoes, and carry them to the shoe room, where I hang up my coat, grab a cushion and a blanket, and head to the meditation hall.

It's warm inside the building. Even though my body is indoors, I seem to have left my mind outside, shivering in the cold. I realize that I am not present, so I pause at the entrance to the hall. I take a deep breath and can feel my feet connecting to the floor. The second breath allows me to feel the warmth of the space around me. After the third breath, I notice my mind settle back into my body. I smile to appreciate the power of the breath. How fortunate we are to have this tool at the tips of our noses; yet we do not always remember its capacity. We catch it, hold it, shorten it, and forget about it. The gift of the breath is precious when we learn to apply it appropriately.

I enter the hall and take my seat on my cushion in the center of the circular room. I look around, and my gaze softens. The walk was certainly worth the effort. A complete stillness embraces me like a familiar friend while my breath remains in the background, supportive, stable, and at ease. I feel grateful for the opportunity to be here with my breath, connecting the body and mind.

Good morning, Sunday.
Let's meditate.

13

Tradition

There is something remarkable about tradition.

Tradition is a little bit of something that we share with our ancestors and pass on to our children. When we follow our traditions, we experience a bond between the past, present, and future. They could be broad cultural traditions or small family traditions. In Curaçao, New Year's Eve wouldn't be the same without the festival of Pagara, and if you are being "floured" on your birthday, you know that there must be a Jamaican in the room.

As Indians, my family celebrates Diwali, but if you come to our house on Christmas morning, we will be around the Christmas tree in our PJs, having tea, homemade Christmas cookies, and stollen with Dutch cheese. It's never about the presents, but always about being present— sharing memories and cards, laughing, and showing gratitude for each other.

Then there are personal traditions. Mine is
a Christmas letter that I started sending out
about nineteen years ago, not realizing it
would become an annual thing. What's yours?

Good morning, Sunday.
Let's meditate.

14

What Will People Think?

Growing up as a little girl in my community, those four words became all too familiar, haunting my every move. They became the intention, drilled into my mind. What would people think if I didn't follow their norms or expectations? If I didn't do what I was "supposed to" do, say what I was "supposed to" say, or wear what I was "supposed to" wear? This person they called "People" followed me around; her judgment was so critical it confined me to living in my shadow rather than discovering and unveiling my true nature.

As I moved into adulthood, I gradually learned to ask myself: "What do *I* think?" By asking this question, I permitted myself to have an opinion and a voice that mattered. This transition was challenging, as the little voice inside my head was somehow still influenced by the approval of "People." Childhood habits have a way of burying themselves deep in our subconscious.

I became too busy living according to People's expectations, so today I continue to learn who I am, what I want, and my purpose in life. My yoga practice has taught me to refine my intention by asking myself: "How does that make me feel?" When I practice mindfully on my mat, I pause to allow myself to notice the effects of the breath and movement.

When I first started this practice, I didn't feel anything. I focused on the outside and what my posture was "supposed to" look like. I would ignore my feelings in favor of the look. Now I am learning that the practice becomes more meaningful when I shift my focus internally and observe when my mind and body feel balanced and at peace.

I now take this practice off the mat and into my life, and when making decisions, instead of asking myself, "What will people think?" I ask myself how it makes me feel. Does it give me joy, comfort, and stability? Does it connect me to my goodness? Does it make me feel nourished, fulfilled, and free? Does it make me feel like I am serving a purpose?

When the answer is yes, I know that I am living from my true nature, with good and honest intentions, and not with the purpose of influencing what people will think.

To live for validation and "likes" from People is draining and eventually leaves us physically and mentally exhausted. When we live with an awareness of our intention, life flows, becomes fulfilling, and the mind can rest in the feeling of ease, comfort, and stability. We stop living in our shadow and allow our light to shine through.

Good morning, Sunday.
Let's meditate.

15

The Ocean

Our mind is much like the ocean. Sometimes
it's calm and clear, perfect for reflection;
sometimes it's full of activity, choppy and
restless, the sound so loud and noisy that it
keeps us awake. When we manage to fight
the waves and go below the surface, there is
stillness and a peaceful, easy feeling.

Like the waves that come and go, so do our
thoughts if we allow them to flow. I've lived
on islands all my life, just a short drive away
from the ocean. Now I open my eyes every
morning, and the sea is right in front of me,
reminding me every day that no matter how
I feel right now, there is always a stillness
inside of me. How magnificent, how blessed.

Good morning, Sunday.
Let's meditate.

16

Stillness

Today I give gratitude to stillness.

Last weekend I was attending a trade show. In anticipation of not having enough time to send out my Sunday-morning message, I prepared it a few days in advance. On Sunday morning, I opened my notes and accidentally deleted the entire message. Initially, I was in a muddle. It was one of those moments when the rewind button would have been as convenient as the purchase of the book *iPhone for dummies*.
I searched and tried everything to retrieve the message, including examining my "deleted notes" file. It seemed like it was gone forever.

I struggled to rewrite the message; however, recalling the exact words in my panic mode was futile. Finally, I decided to meditate and allow my mind to come to stillness. I settled in and focused on the rhythm of my breath.

With each exhalation, I could feel the tension in my body and mind release, allowing me to let go of all thoughts one at a time until my mind rested in the mantra. Thirty minutes later, when I finished my practice, I started to write. There were the words, stored safely, underneath all the turmoil in my head.

Our mind is full of data. When we are riled up, retrieving this information becomes challenging. It's almost like trying to find a beige pair of sox while the washing machine is still going. If we slowly sift through when we turn it off, the sox miraculously appear. Similarly, when we rest the mind in stillness, we can see clearly and retrieve thoughts and ideas that the mind has set aside. Take a moment to pause and reap the benefits of returning to stillness.

Good morning, Sunday.
Let's meditate.

17

The River

Today I give gratitude for lessons learned from the river.

Last week I went on a river walk. My first step was into a pool of mud. It didn't look attractive; however, I continued with an open mind.
As I kept on walking, I kept on learning, and understood the following lessons:

1. Sometimes life is muddy. Never get discouraged; keep walking. No mud, no lotus.

2. The road can be slippery. Take one step at a time. Make sure one foot is grounded before you move the next: *"Padam, Padam."**

3. Be present and enjoy the beauty around you. When you walk this way again, it will look different. It's the nature of nature to change.

---

*   *Padam Padam* is a Sanskrit saying which means "step by step," or "one step at a time."

4. Try to see things from a different perspective. There are more ways to get around the bamboo tree that has collapsed in the middle of the river.

5. Be aware of what you hold on to. The largest branch isn't always stable. Those grounded rocks may be a better choice.

6. There are times you can follow, and there are times you must lead the way.

7. Believe in yourself.

8. Don't be afraid to ask for help—it is not a sign of weakness; it is a sign of trust. Trust.

9. Be meticulous in your step; the water may be a lot deeper than you think. Be prepared if you want to take the plunge.

10. Be mindful of what you touch; beauty can be deceiving. Not all berries are berry nice.

11. The journey may seem long; however, in the end, the reward awaits. Always be grateful for the journey.

There are so many lessons we learn from taking walks in nature. It is the way the universe teaches us how to walk through life.

Good morning, Sunday.
Let's meditate.

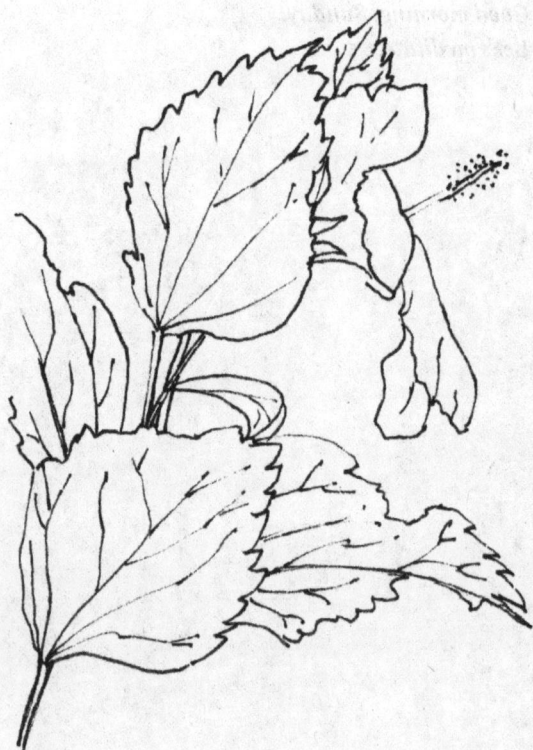

18

Light

There is a hibiscus growing outside my
   bedroom window.
Her corner is dark, and she strives to see
   the sun.
In order to bloom, she turns *outward*
   toward the light and reveals her beauty,
allowing her true colors to shine through.

I sit inside by my bedroom window.
My corner is dark, and I strive to see the light.
In order to bloom, I turn *inward* toward the
   light and witness my beauty,
allowing my true colors to shine through.

Good morning, Sunday.
Let's meditate.

19

The Beach

When my siblings and I were growing up, my mom would take us to the beach every Sunday. We sat under the same tree with the same friends. Mom would put on her very groovy swimming cap with soft multicolor organza flower petals and go for her laps, and we would hang out, chat, take a walk, and swim. Some days we would get to go up to the restaurant and have my favorite lunch: club sandwich and fries.

Today, I have a different relationship with the beach. I love to walk. To hear the waves wash up on the shore, feel the ocean and sand in between my toes, and breathe the fresh ocean air. It clears my head and is therapy for my soul. It's rejuvenating and uplifting. It's my date with nature, just me, myself, and God.

Good morning, Sunday.
Let's meditate.

20

Minimum Daily Requirement

My recommended dietary allowance (RDA)
is the number of vitamins and minerals
I need per day to keep my body healthy
and well nourished. My minimum daily
requirement (MDR) is the least I must do
every day to nurture my mind and soul.
For me, it's a cup of tea at dawn while
reading or watching the sunrise, followed
by a thirty-minute meditation. When I
have more than an hour, I may add some
journaling, a walk in nature, or a yoga
practice. This is my magical foundation.

We all have a different MDR, which changes
during our life span depending on the
attention we place on it and the time we
assign to it. It could be something as simple
as a morning cup of coffee, a brisk walk,

a prayer, or ten jumping jacks. It could
last a few minutes or a few hours, in the
beginning, end, or even in the middle
of the day. It's something that we do
mindfully, daily, that becomes so
ingrained that if we miss it, we feel
incomplete.

Whatever we determine to be our
MDR, may it be that which inspires us
to connect with our true nature so that
we can attend to our day with balance,
clarity, and awareness.

Good morning, Sunday.
Let's meditate.

21

Healing Power Of Sound

At the crack of dawn, I sit on my meditation cushion. In the distance, an owl hoots in a rhythmic, monotonous, yet soothing manner. As the sun rises, several birds start chirping, having simple conversations, adding gentle energy to the early morning.

Gradually the sound of traffic creates some tension in the air. Whether it's the sound of music, nature, or simply the words we choose to use, sound has an interesting effect on our system. When we chant words such as "Om" or "Shanti," we notice a vibration that travels through our system, causing us to feel peaceful and at ease.

On Monday evening, I had the opportunity to experience a "sound bath." After a long day at the office, I arrived at the class feeling tired, overwhelmed, and confused. As I lay on the floor in the room, a talented young lady skillfully extracted various sounds from several bowls, bells, and other instruments. I allowed my body and mind to absorb these variable sounds that traveled through my system. An hour later, I felt as if a tsunami of sound waves had washed every thought and idea out of my head, leaving my mind crystal clear, calm yet energized.

The following day, I noticed a bowl gifted to me by a friend a few years ago on the dresser. It matched the decor in the room perfectly, and I was using it to store my mala beads. I looked frantically for the mallet that accompanied it, hoping our dog hadn't chewed it up. I now have a completely different appreciation for this bowl and its function.

Tomorrow my sound bowl will finally get to sing again.

Good morning, Sunday.
Let's meditate.

22

Listening

I am grateful for the art of listening.

I have a figure of Ganesh on the dashboard of my car. Ganesh is known to be the remover of obstacles. To me, his large ears are a daily reminder to listen more and speak less. While others talk, we are so busy in our mind preparing a response or creating opinions that we often don't listen to what they say. I must admit that I am frequently guilty of this. When we commit to being silent, we learn to sharpen our listening skills. Not only do we listen without judgment to what other people are saying, we learn to listen to the wisdom that resides within us, allowing us to find solutions to obstacles that are beneficial to all.

We can apply the art of listening in other ways, like listening to the tone of our voice when we speak or listening to the vibrations

of the words that we choose and their
effect. There is so much power in sound;
listening allows us to tune in with precision,
like tuning into a radio station and finding
precisely the right frequency. The best gift
you can give anyone is to lend them an ear.
After all, we have two of them, so why not?

Good morning, Sunday.
Let's meditate.

23

Above All The Noise

Above all the noise, there is a place where stillness prevails. A blanket of clouds covers the bustling city below, separating it from the silence of the mountains. Above all the noise, there is no sound, except for the quiet hums of nature. The morning reveals itself with a continuous drop of water clicking as it falls in a steady beat down the gutter on the side of the cottage. It is the residue of the night's rainfall and creates a rhythm set by nature's metronome. Birds tune in with their morning chants while leaves rustle gently as the breeze whispers through them.

For me, it cannot get any quieter than this.

Above all the noise, my mind is clear. It invites me to take a seat on the edge of the mountain to observe the beauty of this planet in its miraculous tranquility. I settle down and notice the cicada's ringing sound, which appears in a wave-like manner interrupting the quiet, much like the petty chitter-chatter that disrupts

my mind, creating irrelevant thoughts. Here, I learn
how nature acknowledges all sounds by giving
them room to ebb and flow without allowing them
to disrupt its peace.

For a moment, nothing matters as everything
pauses to create space and refresh itself from the
bustle of humanity.

The stillness transcends and enables me to close my
eyes and find a place of tranquility within myself in
seconds. A place that is always available yet seems
harder to access amid the noise of the city.

When I head down the mountain to the city today, I
will take a little bit of this silence with me and store
it in my heart so that I can return to it whenever the
noise ascends, and I can remain above all the noise.

Good morning, Sunday.
Let's meditate.

24

The Road Less Traveled

Can I walk the road less traveled,
or do I have to go with the flow?

Can I follow my heart and passion,
or must I succumb to how everything goes?

Can I keep my individuality,
yet feel part of something more?

Can I walk this road less traveled,
so I can find the light of my soul?

Good morning, Sunday.
Let's meditate.

25

The Mountains

Today I give gratitude to the mountains.

It's a little after sunset. My husband and I tried to get in earlier but took a wrong turn and delayed our arrival. We are staying in "Tree," a white wooden cottage at Strawberry Hill, tucked into the Blue Mountains in Irish Town, Jamaica.

It's our little treehouse. The antique four-poster bed sits in the middle of the room, surrounded by white serpentine windows and fretwork panels above the doors, adding charm to the cottage. The never-ending drive on the winding uphill road calls for an early dinner, a glass of Pinot Noir, and a long nap.

At dawn, I step out onto the cool wooden floor of our small square balcony and admire the view from 3,000 feet while sipping my cup of hot Blue Mountain coffee. Crisp, clean air fills my nostrils. This is heaven. In the distance, I see the city of Kingston. Little white buildings of different heights cluster along the shoreline of the Caribbean Sea. Around them are the mountains, bursting with vegetation. I wonder why they call it the Blue Mountains, as all I can see is a palette of many shades of green. It's quiet up here. The only sound is that of the breeze caressing the leaves.

At sunrise, I hear the birds having their morning chatter, ruffling the blanket of silence. There are various species up here; I can tell by the distinctive sounds they make. Noticing this persuades me to listen skillfully to distinguish the twitter. As I scan the trees surrounding my balcony, I wonder if they are "people-watching" me. I could stay here all day but decide that a morning hike could nourish my soul. Another day in paradise is on the horizon.

Good morning, Sunday.
Let's meditate.

26

Letting Go

Dawn is my most favored time of day. It is nature's
way of promising that a brighter day is on the
horizon. In times when I am feeling low, I watch
the sunrise to lift my spirits. This morning was one
of those days, as yesterday another Zoom funeral
of a beloved aunt drained my energy.

When the universe brings us life, we rejoice and
celebrate. However, when the universe retrieves
a life, we question and lament. We forget that
life does not belong to us; it is a gift to enjoy and
return when the lease is up. Letting go of loved
ones continues to be one of the most challenging
tasks that we face in our lives, as attachment
restricts us from separating. When nature forces
us to let go of something or someone when we
are not ready, we seek comfort in holding onto
memories and finding gratitude. Memories fill the

emptiness we find in our soul and help us to move on gradually. Gratitude allows us to be thankful for having had the opportunity to experience love and be loved.

Some mornings, even the moon has a hard time letting go as she lingers in the background holding on to her evening sky. Until the last few seconds, when even she has to let go to allow the rays of the sun to shine.

Good morning, Sunday.
Let's meditate.

27

Intuition

Two weeks ago, on a nature walk in Kempshot, I discovered an intricate spiderweb. The white silk threads were carefully designed, almost invisible to the eye of the spider's prey. Only a distinct angle of sunlight was able to reveal its beauty. The spider's ability to spin a web is innate. She doesn't have to go to web design classes; she simply follows her intuition.

We are all born with strong intuition. Unfortunately, we have cluttered our minds with excessive information and thoughts that obstruct our connection with that which is innate. It's like opening a refrigerator fully stocked with ingredients, and not finding anything to eat. The only way to connect with our intuition is to go beyond the mind's clutter, filled with the noise of judgment and opinion. Once we find that place of silence where intuition resides, we, like the spider, can build a web to catch the gifts that nature has in store for us.

Discover that place of silence and beauty within you to connect with the "aha moments" in your life.

Good morning, Sunday.
Let's meditate.

28

Sharing

Today I give gratitude for the experience of sharing.

I came across a photograph the other day capturing the act of sharing. At the age when feelings of "me and mine" would have been emerging, two toddlers chose to share their fries. At that moment, the intention was genuine and pure. One of my favorite sayings is, "When you have more than you need, build a longer table, not a higher fence." This picture demonstrated this beautifully.

Sharing is not confined to tangible objects, nor is it restricted to items with monetary value. Sharing is something we can all do regardless of material possessions. We all have gifts that we can share with other human beings, such as our knowledge, skills, creativity, patience, love; we can even share a smile. These are qualities that, when shared, multiply and grow within us, reminding us of the abundance of our nature. I would love to share my Sunday meditation practice with you; then, we can share some fries.

Good morning, Sunday.
Let's meditate.

29

Home

There are many places that I have called home. However, Curaçao has a special place in my heart: my first home, my rock, my foundation. I sit here in the early morning, observing the waves of the Caribbean Sea, as I enjoy a cool morning breeze blowing through my hair.

Rocks surround me. They are white, mossy green, cream, brown, and gray. Some are smooth; others are rough, spotted in a light burgundy. They all support each other in one way or another, unperturbed about their differences in size, shape, or color.

As the ocean draws in, I hear a soft rumbling sound and anticipate the noise of the waves crashing against the rocks. My expectations are met within a few moments, and the salty water sprinkles over my knees and toes.

I never took the time to appreciate the beauty
of this tiny island when I was growing up.
I longed to travel and leave this rock, to go to
more exciting places where there was more
to do and more to see. Now, sitting here, I
feel so connected to this piece of wonder, the
rhythm of its music flowing through my veins.
On the edge of this reef, I feel safe and secure.
Can I be strong and stable among the waves
of life's ups and downs, like these rocks?
Can I learn to be still and glisten at sunrise,
allowing my true nature to shine through?

Good morning, Sunday.
Let's meditate.

30

The Attic

In the left corner, I see twenty-nine cans of
paint in various sizes, stacked in an orderly
manner. Among them are paintbrushes, rags, and
unmarked containers stained with rusty handles.
My eyes continue to scan the area. A mattress
lies on top of two rolled-up carpets. Behind it is
a twin headboard that I used in our son's room
when he was eleven, and a plastic container
stores old negatives of captured images from the
nondigital time of our lives. I spot an old white
chest sprinkled with colorful flowers, butterflies,
and a baby-pink trim. I painted it for my daughter
and added her name on the top in pale blue script.
It has served different purposes throughout the
years—a toy chest, dress-up box, art supplies
storage box—and it now contains some books and
projects from her school days. I glimpse suitcases
in all shapes and sizes in the right corner,
collecting dust while waiting for the next voyage.

The attic above our garage is our secluded space
where we store items that we occasionally use,
things that we are not ready to let go of, and
objects we may need one day. The Christmas
decorations have their own space between

the luggage and the metal shelving that holds
the warmers and hurricane lamps. The area is
empty; however, the holidays are over, and in a
few minutes I will return the three boxes and six
trunks of decorations to their assigned space. Our
home, which took a week to decorate, is back to
its pre-holiday look in merely one hour.

The first week in January is a bittersweet time of
year. As much as I love the bustle of December,
a daily schedule looks attractive. Our lives will
go back to their routine after the whirlwind of
holiday parties, beach days, late evenings, and a
house full of family. Just as the items get kept in
the attic, the memories are stored in our mind.
Anytime we desire a memory, we can scan our
mind and find it neatly tucked away. Sometimes
we may have to dig through scattered thoughts or
recognize a scent that triggers a déjà-vu moment.
Other times the memories are right there, waiting
to be retrieved and shared. I glance around
one last time and notice a colorful fabric flower
garland. My father-in-law wore that years ago
at a New Year's Eve party at Coyaba, one of our
favorite spots in town.
I believe I can find a use for that floral accessory.
I pause and smile at the memory of people and
places that are no longer with us but still hold a
unique space in my heart, mind, and attic.

Good morning, Sunday.
Let's meditate.

31

The Daily Practice

It's early Saturday morning, and Winston heads down to the west end of the beach with his rake. He rakes the sand meticulously, one stroke at a time, removing leaves, seaweed, or any debris that the sea has surrendered from the previous night. His technique creates a fan-like sweeping edging from one end of the beach to the other. I admire his patience and his ability to give this mundane task his full attention. As he approaches, I can hear the rake's scratching sound moving rhythmically through the sand, accompanying the ocean waves caressing the shore. Winston has been working here for fourteen years. This is his morning meditation. In a few hours, footsteps will disrupt the pattern he imprinted in the sand. By the end of the day, waves will have washed over and erased every stroke Winston so diligently created.

It's early Sunday morning. A rooster has been crowing for the last hour, as if nature forgot to turn off the snooze button. Winston wakes up and heads to the beach. Once again, he picks up his rake and starts from scratch, raking one stroke at a time. Once more, I am sitting in meditation on my blanket at the other end of the beach, allowing the mantra to sweep my mind. This is my morning routine. By the end of the day, my mind will be cluttered with many thoughts and unnecessary chatter; however, the clarity I receive after my morning practice is invaluable. I hear the rake dragging smoothly through the sand, moving toward me. Winston has come to the end of his meditation, and I have come to the end of mine. I glance up and smile. The beach looks impeccable, and my mind is clear, ready to face a new day.

Good morning, Winston.
Thank you for raking the beach today.

32

The Plunge

Today I give gratitude for being able to choose to take the plunge, or not...

How do you approach the ocean? Do you jump right in? Or do you take small steps and ease in slowly? When I walk into the ocean, I take small steps. I start with my toes, get my feet wet, then my shins, knees, and thighs. I wade there for a moment. I ease down to the waist, and after a bit of splashing, I gradually sink to my shoulders. Then, I dive in and swim.

Interestingly, I approach life in a similar manner. I am not the kind of person to jump in to anything without carefully thinking it through or planning it out. I slowly navigate my life and mindfully calculate the pros and cons before I decide. Once I have made up my mind, I am fully committed. I sometimes wonder if I overthink.

Life could be more intriguing if I stepped out of my comfort zone and just jumped in. Perhaps it would be refreshing if I was more spontaneous instead of cautious and meticulous. Maybe sometimes I could be adventurous and take the plunge.

What about you? Do you test the waters? Or do you jump right in?

Good morning, Sunday.
Let's meditate.

33

Patterns

Today I give gratitude to patterns.

As I walk along the south coast, I pause to admire the ripples in the sand. Like a fingerprint, they identify themselves by leaving a pattern on the planet, only to be disturbed by wind, waves, or footprints treading through their grooves.

I glance at my fingerprint, which is unique to me. It can magically unlock doors and electronic devices, allowing me to enter by merely touching an assigned surface. It's my stamp that travels with me wherever I go. Unlike the ripples in the sand, my fingerprint will remain unchanged. The impression it leaves is my mark in this lifetime.

Although I am not in control of my fingerprint, I can control the patterns that I choose to develop in life. Which one do I want to keep, and which one do I want to discard? Some patterns are so ingrained by habitual behavior that it may take wind, waves, and footprints to disrupt them. Inner strength is required to endure such a transformation.

As I sit this morning in my meditation, I reflect on the patterns I want to impress on this lifetime. How can they be of benefit? What design will I create to urge someone to pause and admire the ripples that I leave behind?

Good morning, Sunday.
Let's meditate.

34

Exploring The Light

The flight to New York (NY) is packed, quite different from a few months ago when airlines struggled to fill their seats due to the Covid-19 pandemic. While boarding, I notice that all the window shades are drawn, allowing the aircraft to remain cool while on the ground. The rays of the sun attempt to penetrate with little success. I settle in, and snooze during take-off.

When I open my eyes, we are well on our way and thousands of feet in the air. I notice that most of the shades are still drawn, and the lighting in the cabin is dim even though the sun shines brightly outside. Around me, passengers are glued to their screens. A young girl is sitting beside me watching an animated movie, one of the free offerings onboard. Her younger sister, Izaria, occupies the window seat. Izaria carefully lifts the window shade to peak outside, inviting in the glare. Promptly, her sister asks her to close it. Izaria's curiosity keeps drawing her to the white clouds that look like marvelous fluffy pillows floating in a bright blue sky, so close that she can almost touch them. Below us, the blend of turquoise-blue colors of the Caribbean Sea enhances its cool and refreshing nature. Izaria closes her shade and begins to nibble on her Cheez-Its while watching "Tom and Jerry." Her mind continues to be drawn outside, eager to explore her imagination, with one eye on her sister and the screen and the other on the window shade.

I remember being in that seat many years ago as a child. Those were the days when all the window shades were open, inviting in the light. We would fight to get the window seat as it was always the most appealing. I would stare outside, admire the planet's beauty, and look for images in the clouds. Today everyone seems to be drawn to the glare of screens rather than the glare of the sunshine.

Izaria slowly lifts the shade again, this time only two inches, hoping that her sister won't notice. Unfortunately, her hopes are crushed, and it looks like this will be a long, shady flight for her.

We are now two hours into our journey. In the aisle across from us, a passenger sits by the window. She is reading on her phone. Her window shade is entirely open, and she is enjoying a glass of red wine. Occasionally, she takes a break to sip her wine and look outside. I glimpse over and take a picture to explore the play of light with the filters on my camera. Izaria glances across, perhaps imagining what it is like to be sitting at that window seat. Maybe one day, she too will be able to munch on her Cheez-Its in Seat 2A while enjoying the view and allowing the sunlight to shine in.

Good morning, Sunday.
Let's meditate and find the light within.

35

Passion

Today I give gratitude to passion.

When we do what we love and love what we
do, it shows in our actions. As we proceed with
love, dedication, and passion, we find a magical
connection that carries us through to completion.
It is visible in our practice, education, careers,
hobbies, and service. Passion can emerge even
in the smaller tasks that we accomplish, such as
preparing a meal for ourselves, walking the dog,
or decorating our Christmas tree. When our
efforts are pure, and we proceed with passion, the
universe acknowledges us in numerous ways.

Sometimes we may get publicly rewarded for
what we achieve with our actions. We may receive
an award, a trophy, or be selected by Forbes as
a top young entrepreneur in our field and age
group. Other times the reward may be subtle.
It could be a meaningful hug, a compliment, or

a thank you note from someone we helped or inspired. Whatever the form of recognition is, the rewards are all significant as each one gives us a deep sense of gratitude.

The pride we feel is because we have given it our all, with our heart and soul. The glow we experience is that of appreciation of the power and energy within us and our ability to find the connection.

At times, we may not even see the results in our lifetime. We should never allow this to discourage us, as the passion lies in the effort, not in the expectations of the outcome. When we plant seeds of love, the results can only be lovely.

Good morning, Sunday.
Let's meditate.

36

My Dog

Today I give gratitude to my dog.

Surya can be feisty, yet I am so fond of this
little ball of terror. She is always excited
to see me, whether I am coming home
after work, from a morning walk, or a long
trip. It's a joyous celebration when I walk
through the door. She runs around the house,
jumps, barks, and squeals, and kisses are in
abundance. Many days when I sit down to
meditate, she will stay right by my side. She is
my biggest fan, and I am the star of her show.

My responsibility is to care for this soul. The
gratitude I receive in return is immeasurable.
She is devoted and teaches me what true love
is. She reminds me that I, too, have access to
this love deep inside me, as it slowly reveals
itself whenever I spend time with her.

The feeling of being loved unconditionally is the most beautiful experience of acceptance and nonjudgment. When we can love all of humanity in this way, our purpose in life is fulfilled.

Good morning, Sunday.
Let's meditate.

37

The Orchid

I live in a small garden where I arrived as a seed.
Every sunrise and sunset, I drink as I need.
Some days impeccable water falls from the sky,
a cool breeze accompanies as the heavens oblige.
On other days, the garden hose distributes in waves
throughout the front yard, all bow and obey.

Surrounding me are beautiful plants, flowers, and trees,
orchids in white, pink, red, orange, and green.
All elegantly glowing, with water beads on their petals
like crystal pearls reflecting in the sun as they settle.
I hope to grow to be as magnificent as them;
however, I cannot see myself as my vision is dim.

Thus, I try my utmost to maintain my equilibrium,
so I can grow to be as exquisite as the Oncidium.
As I increase my expectations and compare myself
    with others,
I get discouraged and doubtful and submit to be covered.
I question the water's benefits and consider my weakness.
However, I remain persistent in my efforts to progress.

For the others remind me I am as bright yellow as the sun,
With speckles of red envied by everyone.
This morning a little girl strolled around the garden in glee.
She marveled in awe and paused in front of me.
For a moment, I glimpsed my reflection in the corner
   of her eye,
I could finally see myself, and I cannot tell a lie.

How much had I grown, how beautiful had I become!
I was one with nature, in harmony with everyone.
For a moment, I experienced truth and bliss,
and glowed in gratitude for this wonderful gift.
For a moment, I saw what everyone saw in me.
And in a blink of an eye, I was set free.

Good morning, Sunday.
Let's meditate.

38

Nature

I've always loved taking pictures of nature. Driving through Europe on our honeymoon, I would ask my husband to stop, just to take a picture of "the view." Being a Jamaican driver, pulling over on a major highway didn't faze him. "Don't you want me to be in the picture?" he would ask. "Not really." Thus, we have many pictures of mountains, valleys, trees, fields, and cows; I captured them as if I thought I could pack them in my suitcase and take them back home with me.

Now, I still enjoy creating snapshots of nature, but being part of it is much more inspiring. Take a walk in nature; grab a branch as a walking stick. Touch the leaves, dig your hands into the earth, run your fingers through the water, and feel the sand in between your toes. Smell the humidity in the air and stop to appreciate God's painting because tomorrow it will all look different again.

Good morning, Sunday.
Let's meditate.

39

Fallen Leaves

The sun rises to invite me to another pleasant day. I head downstairs to my meditation spot, only to find it covered in leaves that have fallen from the almond tree, which sheds once a year in spring. My first reaction is one of utter annoyance as I now have to clear off all the leaves before I can start my practice. I walk over and start to kick the leaves aside; however, something inside of me urges me to stop.

I pause, bend down, and gently pick up the first leaf. I look closer and notice its beautiful reddish-brown color with hints of orange and yellow. This exact leaf was on the tree a week ago, creating shade for me to do my practice. It served its purpose and is ready to let go and make space for a new one. Who am I to kick it around simply because it is now of no further use to me? I start picking up all the leaves one by one while chanting softly, and a sense of appreciation for them comes over me. I place them carefully in a small pile on the side. This act of leaf-picking becomes a morning meditation as I continue to prepare my space with gratitude and reverence.

We often look at even the slightest obstacles as deterrents to reaching our goal. Instead, they are there to remind us to make our practice practical by giving time and attention to the journey, even if it is simply collecting fallen leaves.

Good morning, Sunday.
Let's meditate.

40

Surrendering Control

There's a succulent growing in the backyard. It's a speck in my garden, insignificant compared to the large Areca palms that tower beside it and the broad landscape that surrounds it. The succulent is undemanding, simply desiring a weekly drop of water. It is healthy and does nothing at all but enjoy the sun when it shines and the rain when it falls. It completely surrenders to the happenings of nature. I planted it two months ago with no expectations as my mind was consumed with daily challenges beyond my control.

A few weeks ago, the rains were heavy, far exceeding the quota that the succulent required. I imagined some hardship and assumed that the succulent would struggle to survive. Thus, I was utterly surprised this morning when I noticed that it had grown substantially and multiplied in these unfavorable conditions. I admired its endurance and its commitment to flourishing even though the environment was challenging. I applauded its ability to be.

I did nothing to care for this plant; however, I attempt to control my future as I believe it is in my hands. I plan, overthink, do and undo, worry, ponder, and strategize, only to find out that I continue to have many unresolved questions and obstacles independent of my actions, as they are managed by a force much larger than myself.

I, too, am just a speck in this vast universe.

I can set intentions, direct, plan, and hope; however, ultimately, I am never in control of the sun, the rain, or the bigger picture. I can only learn to be present and find the beauty in every circumstance by discovering a way to shine through it all so that when the storm passes, I too will flourish like the succulent in my backyard.

Good morning, Sunday.
Let's meditate.

41

The Breath

I am breathing in
I am breathing out
I am breathing in
I am breathing out

I repeat these words mentally as I inhale and
exhale. It is an exercise I do when I start to feel
anxious or when my mind fills up with unnecessary
thoughts that are insignificant or unproductive.
I use this technique not to suppress my thoughts
but to release them with the exhalation and avoid
mental clutter, allowing clarity to prevail.

I am breathing in
I am breathing out
I am breathing in
I am breathing out

As the world returns to work after the pandemic, I
gradually prepare to reopen the business. At first,
a sense of hope arises. I am excited and feel like
rejoicing. Then, fear creeps in with moments of

self-doubt. Can I do this? Can I walk out the door with confidence in these unpredictable times? I hesitate and shut the door.

I am breathing in
I am breathing out
I am breathing in
I am breathing out

I hear my neighbor's voice: "Go lay down; put your feet up!" He is yelling at his mother, who refuses to wear her hearing aid. I am inclined to follow his instructions but realize that they are not meant for me.

I am breathing in
I am breathing out
I am breathing in
I am breathing out

I remember how insecure and nervous I was when I taught my first yoga class in 2014 and how grateful I was when students showed up. I recall how elated I was after my first article got published last summer, yet how difficult it was to start the first sentence.

I am breathing in
I am breathing out
I am breathing in
I am breathing out

I know it's not going to be easy, and that life will be different. I will have to make tough decisions and accept the changes they bring. The future remains uncertain, and I can only trust in my ability to get through a challenging year. I know if I take one step at a time, the road will not be overwhelming.

I am breathing in
I am breathing out
I am breathing in
I am breathing out

The breath is my strength to face any obstacles. It is my support that I rely on when life gets too complicated. My mind starts to settle as fear surrenders and courage returns. I look ahead and walk out the door.

I can do this because
I
can
breathe.

Good morning, Sunday.
Let's meditate.

42

Solar Panels

I stand out on my balcony overlooking solar
panels balancing on the red clay rooftops
as they capture the light of the sun blazing
down. While I smother myself in sunscreen to
protect my skin from the damaging rays, the
panels yearn to transform the light into energy
that we can use.

Nature overflows with gifts; it is up to us to
discover how to use them efficiently without
destroying creation.

As humans, our desires urge us to possess the
things we see that we love. We stroll through
the garden, pick the flowers, walk on the
beach, and take some shells home. The flowers
wilt away in a few days, and the shells get
tucked in a drawer as nature watches silently.
We continue to want, possess, and hold on to
things we need and don't need.

The panels take the sun's rays without disturbing it, as the sun continues to share all its glory. It remains unchanging, even though it keeps on giving and continues to be generous with its light.

Can I be like the sun and share my light without becoming dim? Can I maintain my energy as I age without feeling depleted?

How can I be like the solar panels and transform my energy into something beneficial to all without destroying, distressing, or contaminating the source I receive it from?

So many thoughts wander through my mind as I prepare for my meditation. Maybe after I sit in silence, the answer will reveal itself.

Good morning, Sunday.
Let's meditate.

43

Beauty

It's 6 a.m. and I head down to the beach. It's still, dark, and quiet, except for the soothing sound of the waves kissing the shoreline. I spread my Mexican blanket out on the fine white sand facing the ocean, and notice a peculiar glow in the distance. It seems a bit strange since I am facing the west, so I pause in wonder—moments later, the full moon peaks out through heavy clouds that have settled above the horizon.

I am astonished as the beauty of nature reveals itself, and I admire the moon as it sets at sunrise. The dictionary describes dawn as the beginning or rise of anything. However, this morning I observe the moon welcome dawn as her time to rest. She has reflected all night, and now it is time to call it a day.

There are moments when we can catch a glimpse of something unusual in nature. Make the time to stop and witness real beauty unfold.

Good morning, Sunday.
Let's meditate.

44

Sound

A dear friend asked me the other day: "Is it the bird that makes the chirp, or the chirp that makes the bird?"

Every bird has a distinguished sound that it can adjust to suit its environment or its message. When we hear a chirp, we can identify the type of bird because we recognize the chirp. Or, with technology, we can download the app Shazam for Birds on our phone.

We all travel with a sound. Sometimes we try to adjust our sound by changing our environment. We may retreat to the mountains or the seaside for more peaceful surroundings. This is a temporary modification that can be helpful. However, our authentic sound originates from within. When we want to change our sound, we start by changing the quality of our thoughts. When we quiet the mind from the unnecessary noise and chatter and allow our sound to come from stillness, our mind will feel more settled, and our chirp may be a bit chirpier.

Good morning, Sunday.
Let's meditate.

45

Me

Today I give gratitude to Me.

I put on my costume and makeup, disguising myself
with random items I found in the large brown tweed
suitcase stored in the attic. It's Halloween, and I can
be anyone I choose to be—for this one day, it will be
considered entirely appropriate behavior. Children use
this day as an opportunity to indulge in candy. Adults
use it to socialize, de-stress, be silly, and escape from
reality for a day. I take one last glance in the mirror
to put on the finishing touches and notice a stranger
looking back at me. Only the eyes seem familiar.
Perfect! I'm ready for a night of trick-or-treating.

A flood of people enters our neighborhood. Some have
beautiful royal costumes adorned with jewels, while
others pretend to be their favorite superheroes. A little
girl reminds me of the importance of rain clouds, and
a rock star hands me her microphone to sing a tune.
We have scary spectacles like Dracula, ghosts, and
witches, with intimidating demeanors. They all walk
up one by one requesting candy for their treat bags.
I ask the big question—"Who are you?"—expecting

them to know the answer. Some reply confidently, while others give me a blank stare and silently open their treat bags demanding more candy, which is the ultimate goal of the evening.

I pause and smile. Do we really know who we are?
Or does our appearance identify us?

I observe as people react to the costume rather than the person who lives inside. We smile at the princess and admire her beauty. We frown at Dracula, who frightens us with his large fangs. We focus on the exterior and fail to see the person. If we wear the costume long enough, we may even start to believe that this is who we really are.

After an evening of tricks and treats, enjoying my alter ego, I return home. I change into my PJs, wash my face, and look in the mirror. A sense of relief comes over me as the familiar eyes smile back, reminding me that no matter what my body looks like, my true Self is the comfort I yearn for.

I promise to recognize others by looking into their eyes, rather than judging them by their appearance, which changes daily. I will connect with the person living inside the costume, the part that defines who they really are.

Good morning, Sunday.
Let's meditate.

46

Injuries

I am grateful for every injury that I've had
to endure. Over the last eight years, I've had
several minor injuries. They have all been
reminders to move with more awareness,
avoiding fear, which is always lurking and
waiting for the opportunity to control the
mind. When I hurt my sacroiliac joint, I had
to stay away from many of my favorite yoga
postures to allow the healing process. "At least
I can still do downward-facing dog," I thought;
years later, I injured my wrist.

After each injury, I found an alternative way
to start my day, which I learned to love. When
I couldn't do many yoga postures, I discovered
Pilates and spent more time in meditation.
Each injury was a blessing in disguise and an
opportunity to grow. Just as we learn from
our mistakes, so do we learn from our injuries.

We don't give up; we learn to adjust, find
solutions, and move on. The real injury
is getting too attached to our likes and
dislikes, not accepting the certainty of
impermanence, or giving in to fear and
losing control of the mind. As I continue
the aging process, I am reminded that there
are 100 ways to do anything, so when one
way doesn't work for you, try a different
option, but never, never give up hope.

Good morning, Sunday.
Let's meditate.

47

Nature's Little Miracles

A few weeks ago, I witnessed a turtle-hatching in Oracabessa. A mother turtle had laid her eggs and left her nest; her job was done. The little warriors were now on their own. I stood by in awe, watching 138 hatchlings as they paddled their way through the wet sand in a race on the beach, and finally got swept up by the ocean for their first swim.

Some of them were quick and walked with energy. They were on a mission and knew exactly what they were supposed to do. I admired their focus and confidence as they trod fearlessly toward their goal. Others were slower, taking one step at a time. They would pause to rest, taking a moment to catch their breath and climb over some bumps in the sand, which to them must have seemed like mountains. They had courage and determination, never once looking back on their journey to freedom.

The reason for our presence was to deter any predators and ensure a safe crossing for the turtles to the shore. I stood by cheering them on with words of encouragement; however, the journey was one they made on their own, moving faithfully toward the light. In about fifteen minutes, every one of them made it to the vast ocean, swimming away like tiny specks of hope drifting to infinity.

As the salty seawater quickly washed out their sandy eyes, the baby turtles were off on another adventure. Only a handful of them would make it to adulthood, as the dangers of the world are many. The females that survived would come back to this same beach where they took their first steps, to lay their own eggs to repeat the cycle. As with all nature's lessons, this was one to remember and contemplate. We are all little turtles trying to survive in this perilous world; all we need to do is find our path and focus on the light.

Good morning, Sunday.
Let's meditate.

48

Goodbye

When I say goodbye,
look me in the eye.
Be present here and now,
no regrets as years go by.

When I say goodbye,
look me in the eye.
Show me your genuine smile,
your warmth, your soul; don't be shy.

When I say goodbye,
look me in the eye.
We may never meet again,
you will never question why.

Good morning, Sunday.
Let's meditate.

49

Aging

"How old are you?" I ask a little girl who sits next to me on the airplane. Her eyes sparkle as she holds up her six fingers, revealing a huge smile and two missing teeth. "Six!" she exclaims. She seemed happy to be acknowledged, unperturbed that I questioned her age. Children look forward to aging. They are proud to let everyone know how old they are. Every birthday is a celebration, with cake, ice cream, and fun. They admire adults for their abilities, knowledge, power, wisdom, and sense of style, and they love to play "grown-up," as they anticipate becoming adults with all the adventures it entails.

At what point does aging become something we resist rather than look forward to? We tell children that it's not polite to ask adults how old they are, yet it's acceptable to ask a child the same question. When does it become insulting to question someone's age? When we learn to focus

on the benefits of aging, we can accept the challenge
of the change. We can look forward and prepare,
rather than looking behind us with regret. There is
still so much to do, so why not continue to enjoy
our itinerary?

Yes! I do want all my candles on my cake next year,
even if they melt all the icing.

Yes! I do want to celebrate another year of life and living.

Yes! I do want to tell you that I am fifty-nine years old
and am not embarrassed to admit this.

I have some wrinkles, some aches and pains that I
have collected along the way. I can't always remember
your name, and I still take notes with pen and paper.

I am learning to love who I am. I am learning to
appreciate my whole being as it matures. I am wiser,
and I am free. Free from judgment, free from doing
things to impress other people, free to let go of things
that don't serve me anymore. I am free to be me and
to love myself and every part of me.

Good morning, Sunday.
Let's meditate.

50

Nature Walks

Driving in the hills of Jamaica is always an adventure. Sharp turns and bumpy roads are typical, accompanied by many moments of gratitude when no other vehicles are requesting to share the single lane. After a picturesque ride up a narrow road in Port Antonio, we spot a sign tucked away on the right-hand side, revealing our destination: Nonsuch Falls. Its peculiar name draws our attention. We park the car in front of a wooden, bubblegum-pink shack on the side of the road and follow our guide, Tami, down a secluded driveway to the start of our nature walk.

The rainforest has its way of welcoming us, as it lays down a carpet of diverse auburn leaves, fallen twigs, and a variety of rocks. Our first few steps are hesitant as we acclimatize ourselves to the texture of the pathway. Luckily, we all have sturdy walking sticks to assist with balance while confirming the strength of the surface. We continue to follow the freshly cut trail, frequently stopping to admire the various tropical plants and trees. Puppy, the neighborhood dog, decides to join us on our morning hike. He is a natural and appreciates the company.

After fifteen minutes, we reach the top of the river and enjoy the first reward of the journey. A plunge in cool spring water feels refreshing and prepares us for what lies ahead. I now know why we call Jamaica the land of wood and water. Tami reminds us that this is just a sprinkle, so we gather our courage and continue.

The walk is more challenging than I expected, and familiar words of impatience cross my mind: "Are we there yet?" I pause, as I sense fear and hesitation arising; however, Tami is encouraging and reassures me that I am doing well. She pauses with me while I take a moment to be present. I walk mindfully, taking one step at a time, ensuring that my feet are firmly placed.

Puppy is unable to jump across the large rocks connecting the opposite sides of the riverbanks. He cries and howls, begging us to carry him, but we can barely cross the ravine ourselves, so he turns back. My mind tells me that he is the wise one, and once again, discomfort tries to take control. The birds, tree frogs, and rushing water in the distance provide the perfect acoustics, inspiring me to move on. I grab my walking stick; like a mantra, it keeps me steady and focused on my path.

Finally, we get a glimpse of the prize. I stop to catch my breath, and the view takes it away, tempting me to go on. In a few minutes, after climbing over some treacherous rocks, we are welcomed by water cascading down 300 feet into a natural pool. Without hesitation, we jump in and collect our reward for the strenuous journey. The water feels invigorating. I look around, fully expecting a helicopter to arrive and take us back to the top. Tami laughs and assures me that the walk back up will be a lot easier. She gained my trust by believing in me and showing me my potential. I feel confident, gather up my strength and walking stick, and head back to the top.

Nature walks are reminders of how to live our lives. When we learn to take one step at a time, pause for gratitude, face our fears and doubts, trust those who believe in us, and use our practice to support and guide us, the journey has many rewards. Relish them.

Good morning, Sunday.
Let's meditate.

51

That Gut Feeling

My grandfather left India, got on a boat, and sailed to the other side of the world. He had heard that the Caribbean was an excellent place to make a living. There was no TV, internet, Google, or social media in his day; he listened to his gut (maybe to a friend), got on a boat, and took a chance.

Modern methods of communication have changed how we think, plan, and react. We used to rely on our gut instinct. Now, we are forever googling and clicking, influenced by thousands of opinions, likes, and followers. How can we use these newer methods of communication to our advantage without allowing excessive judgment to get in the way? How can we still trust our gut instinct instead of relying on the opinions of the whole world? Our forefathers lived a simple life, but it was complete. We fill up our lives with so many things; we make ourselves busy so that there is no time to find our gut, let alone listen to it. It seems like today the only time we talk about our gut is when we are going on a diet.

One way to listen to our gut is to pause... and listen. At first, it may tell us to feed it; however, if we are patient, it will give us some feedback.

Good morning, Sunday.
Let's meditate.

52

Nourishment

Today I give gratitude for nourishment.

I rise with the sun every morning—yes, even
on a Sunday and a holiday weekend. Watching
the sunrise nourishes me and gives me time
to be not *by* myself but *with* myself. Being by
oneself connotes a feeling of loneliness; being
with oneself is like spending time with a good
friend. When we speak about nourishment,
we often think about food: what we eat and
drink. However, there is so much more that falls
into this category. Nourishment comes from
everything we take in physically, mentally, and
emotionally through all our senses.

What we see, hear, smell, feel, taste, and think
can nourish or deplete us. It's up to us to be
honest with ourselves and make the choices that
allow us to feel sustained rather than drained.

When the sun rises, it promises a fresh start to a new day filled with light, energy, and resilience. What better time to pause and ask oneself: "How do I feel? What can I do/not do to allow my sun to keep shining?"

Good morning, Sunday.
Let's meditate.

53

The Pause Button

"Take a moment to pause."

I say this all the time when I share my yoga practice, and wish I had learned about it sooner. After reflecting on this word, I realized that I was introduced to it a long time ago. In elementary school, recess was called "pauze" (paawze), which is the Dutch word for "break." However, instead of using our "pauze" to pause, we would run around outside, play games, eat snacks, chat with our friends, scream, shout; we did everything except pause or be silent.

Well, isn't that interesting... did we miss the memo?

Take a moment to pause. To stop, connect with the breath, reflect in between tasks, and notice how you feel.

Good morning, Sunday.
Let's meditate.

54

The Observer

Today I give gratitude to the observer.

I walk to the Jay Street Metro Tech subway. It's
a busy station, and I hope to get a seat on the
F Train. As much as I love jumping in an Uber, it's
more economical and faster to take the subway.
The NY metro is a fascinating place to be the
observer. I slowly walk down the grimy stairs to the
underground world, trying to be mindful in a city
where everyone seems to be in a rush to get to their
destinations. I notice the impatience that surrounds
me and choose to ignore the irritated looks. I'm on
vacation; I can afford to lose track of time.

The train stops, and I get on. I find a seat in the
corner, close to the door. I love watching people
on the train. I become the witness. I see a mother
hugging her toddler on her first day of school.
Three teenagers are chatting about their new math
teacher, and a young man in a red hoody sits in
the window seat, staring out into the darkness
as the train rushes through the tunnel. The lady

beside me is playing Candy Crush, oblivious of her surroundings. The passenger across from me has fallen asleep; her head tips back, and her mouth falls open. I remember hearing a myth the other day that humans ingest eight spiders a year in their sleep. I wonder if I should warn her.

The door opens, and a ragged lady gets on the train. Her blond hair hasn't been brushed in five days, and her skirt and top are frayed. She is hungry and begs for small change to purchase a meal for tonight. Everyone ignores her, including me—typically acceptable behavior on the subway. No one makes eye contact; it's easy when you can look down at your phone. She is anonymous like me, except I have dinner plans.

I recognize that I have something in common with everyone around me. I, too, was once a mother taking my toddler to school on her first day, experiencing that mixed feeling of relief and anxiety at leaving my child with strangers. I, too, was that teenager, happy to see my friends after a long summer break. I, too, have had days when I stare into nothingness and allow my mind to wander into the darkness, and I wonder if I have consumed any spiders this year... I, too, ignored the desperate lady begging for small change. I pause and wonder why I pretended not to look? Was it fear? Opening my wallet on the subway certainly isn't wise. Would I have behaved any differently if I had looked into her eyes and seen her despair? What would a wise person do?

So many thoughts run through my mind. My focus shifts from being the observer of my outside world to observing my inside world. Examining my own actions is challenging. The train slows down, and my thoughts are interrupted: 42nd Street, Bryant Park, it's my stop. The untidy lady has disappeared. I get off the train and walk up the grungy steps into the light of the day, leaving behind the underground and a doubtful mind.

When we strip ourselves of all our titles, we are all the same. We are all anonymous, experiencing this world in a similar way. What makes us different is when we pause to examine our lives and our actions. We can choose the way we respond to situations. We can communicate through a smile, a kind gesture, or handing out a dollar to someone in need. Perhaps next time I get on the F Train, I will prepare and keep a dollar in my pocket in case I see her again.

Good morning, Sunday.
Let's meditate.

55

Birthdays

We all have that desire to feel special, and birthdays
are the perfect time for that. Sometimes we can
be a bit hard on ourselves. Through self-judgment
or trying to improve in every way, we fail to
appreciate ourselves just the way we are. One of my
teachers says: "You are already good; you couldn't
be better. You just have to find your goodness."

Birthdays are the day of the year when you are
acknowledged and appreciated, and no one can
deny you another slice of cake. Remember that
glow on your face when you blew out those candles
when you were just a child? These days I glow even
more as the candles are countless. Some may say
that all this attention will inflate the ego. Share
your cake with all those around you so your ego
won't be the only one to get fed.

Good morning, Sunday.
Let's meditate.

56

The Anchor

It's a windy morning and slightly overcast as I walk down to the beach. It is a cozy alcove, like many of the beaches in the area. A nook carved out in this "baranka den laman" (rock in the sea), as they affectionately call the island.

A fishing boat catches my eye, so I circle to the edge of the rocks. The water is choppy, and the fisherman secures the boat with an anchor. I sit on the edge of the rocks and become the observer. Watching the boat feels like a meditation. As the wind picks up, the water becomes rough, causing the waves to splash over and through the minor cracks in the rock. Hundreds of tiny crabs are running around frantically looking for a place to seek shelter; they must know something that I don't.

I look up and feel a slight drizzle, which suggests the unfolding of some heavy rain. I expect the fisherman to head back to shore; however, he reaches into the stern and grabs a large black cover, which he wraps around himself. He remains seated calmly in the fishing boat, which now looks as if it will crash into the rocks. I am amazed by his courage and the confidence he has in the anchor. The rain picks up, so I run to find a dry spot under a beach umbrella, where I take my seat on the sand and connect with the breath.

We all have something we can use as an anchor as we wait for the storm to pass.

After about fifteen minutes, the rain subsides. The fisherman removes the anchor and heads off to sea. I get up off the sand and return to my room.

Good morning, Sunday.
Let's meditate.

57

Journaling

Thoughts are floating in and out of my mind
as the breath flows in and out of my nostrils.
Some linger long enough for me to take notice;
others float through like a passing ship. I grab
my journal and start to write down those that
seem to be more profound or deserve a little
more of my attention. As I watch them appear on
paper, I sense ease in my mind. Some thoughts
may be things that I need to let go of, as they
serve no purpose cluttering up my head. Writing
them down allows me to release them as if I am
liberating myself from a heavy burden. Other
thoughts expand into strings of words coming
straight from the heart. I watch them bloom
into views worth sharing, and reflect on them
as I continue to explore my mind. The art of
journaling is something we learn by sitting and
being present with our thoughts and emotions.

There are days when I think I will have nothing to write. I pick up my journal, set a timer for three minutes, and start to write precisely that: "There is nothing to write about..." Suddenly words start appearing. They were waiting for an introduction and the opportunity to peek through the curtain and step onto the stage. My three minutes expand into four, then five. The words continue to enjoy freedom as they move swiftly across the recycled paper. I put down my pen and feel complete. My mind is clearer, my heart is lighter, and I am ready to start my day.

Good morning, Sunday.
Let's meditate.

58

Self-discipline

I am grateful for self-discipline, our inner traffic light that keeps us on track. It's so simple: When the light is red, stop; when the light is green, go; when the light is orange, proceed with caution. We all have our built-in traffic light system that tells us when to stop, go, and be cautious. When we don't obey the light, we create confusion. We've all been in that situation at a dinner party when we want to have just one more drink or one more bite, and our traffic light is flashing red: STOP. Yet we disregard the warning and indulge in the pleasure. Other times we see a great opportunity, and our light is flashing green: GO. Yet fear and doubt hold us back and step on the brake.

The next day we play that "shoulda coulda woulda" episode in our head. The orange light is a bit tricky, that gray, in-between area when things are not just black or white. This is when we must dig down deeper and apply discretion. The more we practice stillness, the more we learn to sharpen and refine our discretion and observe the traffic lights within ourselves: our self-discipline. The reward is that life seems to flow more smoothly.

Next time you are at a traffic light, follow the rules; they were created for a purpose. Without self-discipline, life is just one big traffic jam.

Good morning, Sunday.
Let's meditate.

59

Surrender

Surrender is not a sign of weakness. Surrender
does not mean you have to stop living.
Surrender does not mean you have to lie there
like a deadbeat and let everyone walk over you.

Surrender means you have to trust.

We have been told all our lives to be strong,
stand up on our own two feet, have courage,
be independent, and not give up.

It takes courage to surrender. It takes strength
to surrender. It takes power to let go.

I am not asking you to give up. I am asking you
to trust.

To trust in love. To trust in the truth. To trust
in the universe.

We hold on so tight that we cannot let go. We become attached to things, ideas, and thoughts. We even hold on to our breath...

I am not asking you to give up; I am simply asking you to breathe.

It is not easy to surrender. I practice it every day as I surrender to my mantra and allow it to take me to the depths of my being.

Surrender to the truth, surrender to the breath, surrender to the mantra, and allow it to show you the way.

Good morning, Sunday.
Let's meditate.

Attend ^{to} the Action

Attend to Action

Attend Action

Attend-tion

Attention

60

Being Present

How do we practice being present? When we can give our full attention to what we are doing, we experience beauty in motion. Last week I went to a meditation retreat where the service I was assigned to do was to dust mindfully. I thought that it was an easy task, as I do enjoy cleaning. I started zipping through the motion and quickly finished the first room. "Are you done?" asked Rosa, who was in charge. "How was your experience?"

Well, to be honest, I didn't really pay attention to how my experience was. Was it a dusty one? Not so dusty one?

"Did you feel the connection between the duster and the surface?" Rosa continued.

I realized then that the task was not simply to dust but to be in the moment and live it fully. When we live in the moment, we learn to appreciate every detail in front of us. Most days, we are on automatic pilot. We wake up, brush our teeth, and go through our daily routine. Our mind drifts here and there, planning the day, and thinks about everything except what we are actually doing. When our body is in the shower, our mind is in the car. When our body is eating breakfast, our mind is focused on the news. And so life passes us by one day at a time. When we look back, we don't know where the time went because the mind was so busy wandering around in rewind or fast-forward mode that it wouldn't even notice if time stood still.

When we train the mind to attend to the action with full attention, the mind gets fully absorbed and experiences life with love.

Dusting was simply a way to practice giving one-pointed attention. The real task is to apply this practice to our daily lives so that every action is done with intention, and everything we do serves a purpose.

Good morning, Sunday.
Let's meditate.

61

Signs From The Universe

It was 6 p.m. I had half an hour to be home and three errands to run. I was feeling ambitious and decided I would do all three. I picked up an item in the busy grocery store. Lines were long, so I headed to the "ten items or less" line, expecting it to be the fastest choice. After five minutes, I was still in the same spot, with less patience than I started with. "Oh my God, I thought this was the express line," I commented. A stranger in front of me turned around and smiled: "Always say nice things," he remarked, "maybe she is new."

It was like a message from the universe to see things from a different perspective and find my patience. I smiled and immediately felt a shift. I realized that he was right; being impatient was

only causing me to get frustrated, disturbing
my peace of mind. I needed to adjust my
attitude. The situation would not change, so
I had to either wait patiently or prioritize my
errands if I still wanted to be on time. I decided
that the other two errands were more critical
and being late was not an option. I could come
back to the supermarket in the morning when I
had more time.

The universe is always sending us messages in
different ways, some more obvious than others.
It is up to us to be tuned in and recognize
them. Everyone and everything in front of us is
our teacher.

Good morning, Sunday.
Let's meditate.

62

To Serve

I am grateful for the opportunity to serve those
who are less fortunate. My visits to the children's
home are a huge reminder of the importance of
gratitude. The children love to hug you when
you walk in, their hearts just craving attention
and reassurance. I'm always amazed at what
makes them happy. It's those little things that
are so available to us that we take for granted:
playing a board game, making holiday cards,
reading a book, blowing bubbles, or just asking
the children for their opinion so that they feel
that they too matter. Children are our future;
why not make a difference in their lives by
giving them a little bit of your time? In return,
you receive the best gift you could ask for: love.

Good morning, Sunday.
Let's meditate.

63

Humility

In a world driven by money and fame, by rewards, recognition, ratings, and "likes," it is easy to get caught up in our ego and challenging to maintain humility. Humility is comfortable; it's when we are being ourselves, offstage with no makeup and our hair up in a ponytail. It feels so good to be in our own skin and feel grateful for who we are without all the labels and attachments. Humility is the ability to be in costume and still be that same person we were backstage, rated G, for all to see. Some cultures have humility embedded in their greeting; a bow of the head is all that is said, as a gentle reminder that after all, we are all one.

Good morning, Sunday.
Let's meditate.

64

The Spirit Of Wonder

I went for a walk this morning with my dog, Surya. The sky was a clear blue, and the air was crisp and cool. My intention was to get some exercise, and hers was to rediscover the neighborhood. At first, I walked her, making short stops at selected places that I knew she often visited. I could sense that my choices of stops and direction were not up to her expectations, as at times she would tug at the leash and resist moving on.

After fifteen minutes, I decided to let her walk me and lead the way instead. Our pace slowed instantly, as she frequently paused to smell the grass and the bark of the many trees. I wondered what she was noticing that was different from yesterday or the day before.

It would be interesting to read her blog. She lulled a lot and thoroughly enjoyed her walk while I practiced my patience as I allowed her to linger a little longer. We walk this neighborhood frequently, and as lovely as it is, I become oblivious to the minor changes in the foliage when I don't pay attention. On the other hand, Surya seemed to discover it as if she was walking here for the first time. Every tree for her was intriguing, and her curiosity grew as she happily strolled along.

How refreshing it is to be able to rediscover newness in something routine. To see beyond the mundane and revive it to enliven your spirit, to see each day with fresh eyes. To linger a little longer with attention so you can rediscover something new every day as if it were your first. To invite the spirit of wonder to wander with you.

Good morning, Sunday.
Let's meditate.

65

Commitment

When we commit to something, we make a promise. We sign a deal, are steadfast and determined. We may plant a seed in fertile soil; however, without the proper follow-up, it will not flourish. Commitment is the water that allows the seed to germinate and grow. It is a practice.

As human beings, we are capable of a lot of things. Some of them, we would have never imagined possible. These could be positive actions as well as negative actions. Therefore, it is wise to contemplate the value and consequences of what we are committing to when we decide to commit. What is our desire? Why do we want this? Is it valuable to us? Will it benefit or harm others?

Once we have contemplated its purpose, it's
a matter of execution and sticking to it, being
mindful that the results may not always comply
with our expectations. Drop the expectation,
give it 100%, and stay committed.

Think of something you love to do or a quality
that you admire. Embrace it.

Commit with passion.

Commit without judgment.

Commit to succeed.

How do we become runners? Run every day.

How do we become kind? Practice kindness
every day.

How do we become meditators? Meditate
every day.

Good morning, Sunday.
Let's meditate.

66

Stay Awhile

I'm on vacation in my home.
These halls do not belong to me.
All my possessions in one small box.
I feel light and free.

I left my baggage at the door,
and walked in with the breeze.
No stuff, no clutter, no pending thoughts,
my mind is clear to see.

I settle in and stay a while,
pour myself a cup of tea.
The children's laughter in the park
reminds me to remain carefree.

I'm exploring the freedom in letting go,
not holding on to what was never mine.
We come in this world not to possess,
but to leave something behind.

I'm on vacation in my home.
The energy here is pure.
Shall I stay or shall I leave?
My bags wait at the door.

Good morning, Sunday.
Let's meditate.

67

A Little Bit Of Nutmeg

It's Friday morning. Jermaine's only concern today is how he is going to feed his ailing mother. He puts on his cap and hopes for the best as he heads out the door. Business has been extremely challenging. Jermaine decided to move his nutmeg stall out of the vicinity of the market to a less crowded area, hoping to capitalize on his exclusivity. His master plan failed when the authorities confiscated his goods, as he chose to operate on private property without permission from the owner.

Nutmeg, an aromatic spice that centuries ago was only found in the kitchens of affluent homes, is now available on every street corner in the city. It is one of those spices used sparingly in recipes—complemented by cinnamon, cloves, or cardamom—so as not to be overpowering. If unavailable, it could easily be omitted from any recipe, as it is not a required ingredient. However, when included, a sprinkle adds some zest by enhancing the meal's flavor with nutty nuances.

I glance at my long shopping list while pushing my cart down the aisle in the supermarket. A young man approaches me. He is well dressed and is wearing a baseball cap. He says that he doesn't want any money but asks if I would buy him some soup for his ailing mother from the vendor across the street. I hesitate for a moment, as I am not comfortable with his request to leave the supermarket. I offer to purchase the ingredients for soup and suggest that he prepare the soup for his mother when he returns home. His eyes widen in surprise as he confirms my permission to add some items to my cart.

Like adding nutmeg, his portion in my cart is merely a tiny fraction of the total contents. At the checkout, I separate his items and put them in a bag, which I hand to him after loading up my car in the parking lot. He is grateful, as I encourage him not to give up hope and to continue his nutmeg business in approved areas only. I am grateful that I sprinkled a little nutmeg in my day to enhance the flavor of my life.

Good morning, Sunday.
Let's meditate.

68

Feeling Grounded

I stand firmly and feel the earth underneath the four corners of my feet.

I feel balanced, secure, and unshakable. The feeling starts in my body and is slowly absorbed by my mind. I proceed without hesitation, with confidence and decisiveness. This feeling connects me to my spirit, and I sense calm, love, and tranquility supporting my thoughts, speech, and actions.

As the wind blows, I am no longer the leaf that gets tossed around like a feather, indecisive and unsure of whether or not I will tumble and fall.

I am strong, like the trunk of the tree. And even though the rush of the wind may try to blow me over, my branches graciously catch them as I sway to and fro, waltzing with each gust I embrace.

Feeling grounded is a state of mind that allows me to connect with my truth and be comfortable with who I am in my skin—unbound by comparison and unnecessary competition or the need to prove that I am worthy of being. It allows me to close my eyes and trust myself.

As I sit on my cushion this early Sunday morning, I am grounded and at ease, knowing that I am free to be me.

Good morning, Sunday.
Let's meditate.

69

Silver Linings

One thing that kept me hopeful throughout the pandemic was the ability to find silver linings. Every day that passed, I told myself that something good would come out of all these restrictions, curfews, and quarantines. At the start of the pandemic, I found myself clinging on to my "normal" life and lifestyle, fearful that I would lose everything I had worked for. I was completely attached to my job, routines, and plans, and could not imagine my life without all these external factors. Anxiety was high, and I discovered that keeping myself busy helped channel my energy instead of living in panic. So I worked from home, reorganized, swept, mopped, Zoomed, had meetings, made lists, made care packages, kept up with the news, called family and friends... there was never a dull moment while we were masked-up and semi-locked down.

As the months passed, however, I learned to pause throughout the madness. To stop and do nothing. When I paid attention, I was amazed at how many gifts were right in front of me, waiting for me to notice them and nurture my soul. Things that I took for granted revealed themselves as silver linings. Some of these were external, such as numerous evenings sitting on the dock sipping wine and watching pelicans, or enjoying my daughter's company as her energy filled our home for six weeks.

I found joy in grounding myself in small projects around my garden and lazing with my dog on the swing. Exploring the island while hiking confirmed the natural beauty of Jamaica. Through reflection and deepening my practice, I saw internal glimpses of those possibilities that become clear only when we can create space in our mind, let go of the past, and trust the future.

Can I find the courage to follow my heart and have confidence in the internal silver linings? If they are as promising as the external ones, I have nothing to lose.

Good morning, Sunday.
Let's meditate.

70

The Sound Of Silence

I am grateful for the sound of silence.

There are different levels of silence. We have the silence of a soundproof room, and early morning in the countryside or by the sea, where you hear the sounds of nature: birds chirping, waves rolling in and out, or the breeze rustling through leaves in the trees. The sound level that humans have added to the equation through inventions and industrialization—our voices, habits, choices, and actions—can be interesting.

Sound varies according to the city, culture, society, and activity. For example, I just returned from spending a week in Switzerland. The first day back home was almost like a shock to my system. Even in the busiest environment, like the Zurich airport or the train station at rush hour, there seemed to be an underlying sense of order and calmness. In the security line, voices were subdued as everyone somehow knew what to do and didn't need to be reminded. In the city, people spoke respectfully in a lower tone of voice.

The experience of being in this type of environment, with a more restrained sound level, allowed me to feel more present, less hurried, and less distracted. Some may feel like this way of life is boring or lacks emotion. To me, it felt grounding and empathetic as it reminded me to be aware of the people around me. Can we live in a city with the hustle and bustle yet still live with compassion, consideration, and presence? At what point does the level of sound become noise?

Everyone has a different tolerance level for sound until it becomes noise. What to some may be noise to others is music to their ears. When we live in noisy environments, we find a way to deal with it by not giving the noise our attention and not noticing it anymore as we learn to tune it out. What else are we tuning out? Noise can be abrasive and nauseating to our system, obstructing the mind from thinking clearly or focusing. Interestingly enough, we have found solutions for this by inventing noise-canceling headphones or creating apps that generate "white noise," where we resort to choosing noise to drown out the noise.

Deep within each of us is a place of silence, a peacefulness that we can connect with. When we live in noisy surroundings, it becomes even more essential for

us to spend time in silence every day, clear our mind,
find our center, and reset. Meditation allows us to tap
into this space, connect with our breath and stillness,
and recharge.

Good morning, Sunday.
Let's meditate.

71

Dancing

Oh, how I love to dance! When I dance, I become
one with music; I am present with every step I take
and feel happy and free. I started ballet classes at
six, as many of the girls in our family did. It gave
us an excellent foundation for dance. My teachers
had a no-nonsense and disciplined approach, yet
we looked forward to our biannual performances
when we got our two minutes of fame on the stage.

When I feel down or stressed out, dancing is the
perfect remedy. I'll put on a favorite salsa tune and
dance by myself, or occasionally I'll even waltz
around the room with my dog. She doesn't object,
so I assume either she likes it or thinks I've lost
it. Yes, for a moment, I have lost it: all thoughts,
worries, and responsibilities.

Good morning, Sunday, shall we dance?
But first,
let's meditate.

72

Planting Seeds

Today I give gratitude for being able to plant seeds.

It was early December, and my front yard needed
a makeover. The garden resembled a pitchy-patchy
combination of random plants, and the tall king
palm in the left corner was interfering with the
power line. I called a landscaper, and she agreed
to assist in the makeover, reminding me that
the results wouldn't be visible until the spring.
We removed some of the existing plants and set
them aside for replanting in other areas. We soon
discovered that the top layer of soil was shallow,
which was probably why my garden wasn't thriving.
She brought in her crew, who dug two feet deep
and filled the area with fresh topsoil and fertilizer.
She then skillfully planted an array of plants that
we chose with intention. We watered, watched,
and waited.

A few weeks later, I noticed some callaloo and sweet
peppers springing up, along with some weeds,

which were not on the list of selected plants. My gardener explained that the seeds were already in the soil when it was delivered. He removed the unwanted weeds and had the callaloo for lunch. Spring arrived, and the garden was starting to look harmonious. I could now see the outcome of the seeds that we planted and enjoy the beauty of the landscaping.

Many seeds are planted in our mind from the time we are born, some with and others without intention. Some die, while others germinate, grow roots, and eventually emerge as plants or weeds. It is up to us to decide which ones we wish to keep in the garden of our mind and which ones we want to eliminate. We can trim back the weeds so that they are hidden; however, they will return until we choose to remove them from their roots so that they will never resurface again. We cannot continue to blame nature for sowing undesirable seeds. Once we are mature, it is our responsibility to examine our thoughts and deeds so that our mind will continue to produce flowers instead of weeds.

Good morning, Sunday.
Let's meditate.

73

Trust

It's 5 a.m. My eyes open, and I witness the thoughts running through my mind. They are in a race. Finance starts, and I begin to wonder where she is heading. I get up before I can see the other participants. I am grateful for the ability to get out of bed and leave the thoughts behind on my pillow, hoping that they won't be there again tomorrow morning.

I start my daily routine, not knowing which day it is. Does it matter? I'm not going anywhere. We are supposed to stay home while coronavirus explores the island. Maybe I'll go to the grocery store. The one place that was a chore going to weekly has now turned into a favorite outing. I brush my teeth, pour myself a cup of hot green tea in my favorite bone china mug, and move out of the cool air of the air conditioning into my daughter's room.

Here, the windows are open, and a fresh early-morning breeze fills the room. It's peaceful and quiet.

I look out at the ocean and watch the first pelicans dive for their breakfast. They live in the moment and trust that the universe will provide them with their needs. I, too, want to trust this way and stop the doubt that slowly attempts to sneak into my mind when I am not present. The pelicans fly with such ease and grace. I've spent hours watching them this week. Although it can't be an easy task to catch their meal, they are precise and accurate, moving through life with poise and composure. As I watch them, I feel reassured that there is freedom in trusting the universe to provide. My mind is once again put at ease.

My time for morning reflection is precious. Some days I read, some days I sit. Today I write. When my teacup is empty, I set my timer without expectations and sit for my morning meditation—thirty minutes of going within. Every day it's a different experience, like the sunrise: No two are ever the same.

I allow my mind to settle and guide it into following the flow of my breath. My day has begun. Today is going to be the best day of my life.

Good morning, Sunday.
Let's meditate.

74

The Silence Within

I take my seat and close my eyes. There is a stillness that runs so deep I can sense the peace within and without. Even time feels like it's still. My body is motionless. As gravity holds it in place, like a magnet drawn to steel, it keeps me calm, my mind at ease. There is nowhere to go and nowhere to be. Except here and now.

I get up mindfully and walk outside. The silence comes with me. I hear my footsteps, one at a time, echoing through space. The stillness remains with me, even though I am moving. The sound of my footsteps walks by my side. I hear a single bird, and then another. They accompany my steps, echoing through the silence. A gentle wind blows. I hear each leaf as it moves separately from the rest. I can single out each sound in its own space. The stillness is with me, allowing me to recognize the stillness in everything.

Tomorrow I will return to this sacred space within. To reconnect with the stillness that I so yearn for, I will take a little piece with me again and again, until one day all the pieces will complete me, and I will be whole.

Good morning, Sunday.
Let's meditate.

75

The Breeze

Today we are having another windy morning.
You can't capture the breeze in a picture; you must
sit and experience the flow of Mother Nature's
breath. The breeze is the long exhalation, like
a sigh of relief after a long, strenuous week of
running around trying to complete one more
thing on the to-do list. Mother Nature, too, seems
to have these days, as she tries hard to recover
from the stress that we put her through.

When our exhalation is longer than our inhalation,
our mind and the nervous system naturally
calm down, allowing the release of unnecessary
thoughts and tension that we habitually hold on to.
I close my eyes and feel: The touch of the breeze
is cool and calming, the sound like a mantra
whispering in my ear. There is so much to learn
from nature: the outdoor classroom created just
for you. So breathe in for four and exhale for six.

Good morning, Sunday.
Let's meditate.

76

Detachment

There are many aspects of attachment. We get attached to people, places, habits, foods, music, thoughts, ideas, expectations—anything that can connect with our senses or emotions. Today I give gratitude for the ability to let go of material things: step one of detachment. As we travel through our lifetime, we accumulate many things. How much of them result from desire, and how much from necessity?

We get tempted by beauty and innovations that draw our attention, stimulate our senses, convince us that our lives will be empty without all these items. It's not until we start packing that we realize the number of our possessions and our bond to them. Are we allowing things to define who we are? Is it fear and insecurity that urges us to hold on? How many things are we keeping in that box, and how many boxes are we keeping with things? As we reminisce and go through the souvenirs of our life, we notice that some of the things we hold on to remind us of a feeling.

A favorite T-shirt that gave us comfort, a notebook from high school reminding us of our hard work and accomplishments...

We may hold on to these for many years as they still bring us a sense of joy when we see them. We lovingly put them back in the box, as the time to let go has not yet come. Other things we accumulate come from pure indulgence, which turns into clutter that takes up more space: the thirty-seventh canvas tote bag you got to save the environment instead of using plastic, the dress you splurged on that will fit you again someday and, hopefully, still be suitable or trendy.

It is not easy to detach ourselves from our possessions; however, when we do let go, we are no longer burdened by the unnecessary weight. We feel light and free as we create space in our lives. As I learn to appreciate and enjoy the things I already have, I am less likely to accumulate the things I do not need. Take a closer look at what you are holding onto. Do you possess it? Or is it possessing you? Can you simplify your life and still enjoy living? This is certainly something to meditate on.

Good morning, Sunday.
Let's meditate.

77

Measure

I placed the nine ingredients and cooking and measuring utensils on the kitchen counter to prep for the meal. It was my first attempt at making risotto. Measure plays a vital role in my kitchen, as cooking does not come naturally to me. However, with a good recipe, some invaluable tips from my daughter, and the relevant measuring tools, I can prepare a feast.

Cooking risotto is an excellent way to practice being present and paying close attention, as it requires you to add stock intermittently as needed while watching the liquid being absorbed as you keep stirring slowly at a low temperature to deter boiling. I added each ingredient at the instructed time while avoiding a sizzle. The timing I used to add each ingredient, the temperature, the speed at which I stirred, and the quantity of liquid added, would all affect the dish's flavor. Determining when to turn off the fire and whether or not to add more liquid required some skill and judgment as I strived to achieve al dente, the perfect balance, and consistency of creaminess, stickiness, and firmness. Some may have preferred to add half a teaspoon more of black pepper or a tablespoon of butter; others may have chosen to reduce the amount of salt. It was a dance of precision.

The kitchen is not the only place to use measure. Life is full of moments that are best in the proper proportions. How long should we sleep? How many hours should we spend at work? What amount of food, liquid, and exercise do we need for a healthy lifestyle? When is the right time to speak, and when should we be silent? The list goes on.

There is no right or wrong answer. The answer is fluid as it changes according to many circumstances, including the time in our lives. In our quest for a life of al dente, a teaspoon of attention will alert us to the imbalance, and the answer arises when we connect to our stillness.

Good morning, Sunday.
Let's meditate.

78

Encouragement

Many of us strive to be independent, strong, and successful in our endeavors, whatever they may be. The confidence that comes from personal accomplishment is uplifting and rewarding.

Although our achievements are gratifying, there is something to be said for receiving encouragement. Having someone who reassures us of our capabilities, or gives us honest feedback, is a reminder that someone believes in us. Moral support is a gift that we can provide to a friend, a loved one, or even a stranger. Some may have a whole fan club; others may have a team. Some of us only need one person to trust in us, remind us that we are capable and that we are not alone.

We are all busy living our lives. Can we take a moment to lend an ear to a friend? Can we give a few words of encouragement to another human being? Can we appreciate the immeasurable power of words of encouragement?

Good morning, Sunday.
Let's meditate.

79

Forgiveness

Do we ever *really* forgive and forget?

I'm not talking about when someone forgets your birthday or steps on your toe. I'm talking about something much larger than that. When someone hurts you so deeply, it feels like the injection you get in your gum at the dentist: It stings like hell, and then you go numb. I know that when I forgive someone, I feel I have let go of a burden that I've been carrying around. It's a sigh of relief. It's the feeling I get after a long exhalation. However, there are instances when a few weeks or months later, resentment sneaks out from its secret cave, causing the emotions to come flooding back.

Did I really forgive? Or was it just in that one moment?

Did I totally let it go? Or was I still hanging onto one loose string? The string of expectation: expecting the other person to change.

When we truly forgive someone, we forgive with no expectations, and we accept the other person the way they are.

When we forgive, we learn *not* to allow our feelings to have control over us. The emotional triggers may still be there, but we don't allow them to be activated.

When we forgive, we don't only forgive once. It is a constant attitude of being able to give up the past. We get peace of mind by giving up the past: We give up wishing that the past could have been different.

Can I forgive and forget?

I can choose to let go of my expectations and my resentment because they belong to me.

I can choose to let go of all loose strings because they belong to me.

I can choose to show up on my yoga mat every day here and now, where the past is not present because I can learn to let go.

Good morning, Sunday.
Let's meditate.

For-Give

For-get

Give up the Past

Get Peace

♡

80

A Walk On The Hill

I was on a mission,
searching for stillness on the hill.
I had fifteen minutes,
time wouldn't stand still.

I started in the kitchen
and moved down the stairs.
I looked in the basement,
along the rows of chairs.

I walked into the garden
and stood below the trees.
I circled the pond
and glanced between some leaves.

I heard some birds chirping,
a woodpecker up ahead.
I saw the goats pausing,
as they left the shed.

I looked down in the valley
and up at the sky.
I paused, closed my eyes,
I found stillness deep inside.

Good morning, Sunday.
Let's meditate.

81

The Space Within

I close the door and go inside. There is a dense
layer of dust from the Sahara Desert hanging in
the air. Like a magic carpet, it floated across the
vastness of the Atlantic Ocean and now lingers
outside my window. The dust is thick and heavy,
resembling a fog, and obstructs my view of the
mountains across the lagoon. The sun lurks in the
background, creating a yellowish haze, and I am
unable to see its usual dazzling light. Occasionally,
a ray peeks through, reminding me that it is
still present. The warm glow is comforting. The
media tells me to close all my doors and windows,
stay inside, and wear a mask for protection if I
venture outside. I remain within, where I am safe.
Tomorrow all will be clear.

I close my eyes and go inward. There is a thick
fog obstructing my view of the Self. It seems to
have layers and layers of thoughts, likes, dislikes,
attachments, fears, and doubt, inhibiting me from

seeing my true Self. My patience grows weary, but I sit and peel away one layer at a time. Some days I get a peek of the light within, reminding me that it is still present. Like a ray of the sun, it shimmers through, and I get a glimpse of the truth. It gives me hope and courage that I am on the right path, even though a haze surrounds me. My mind tells me to let go of the sounds around me and journey inward using the mantra and breath as a guide. I remain within, where I am safe. Tomorrow all will be clear.

Good morning, Sunday.
Let's meditate.

82

Strength

There is outer strength, the body's physical strength, that enables us to lift a heavy suitcase into the overhead compartment. There is inner strength, which relates to the ability to withstand and endure difficult circumstances. It empowers us to be mentally sturdy, stable, determined, and capable. Some call this getting tougher when the going gets tough. However, tough can be hard and rough, what you would want your boots to be when treading through the snow. If we are not mindful, toughness can turn into indifference, bitterness, and resentment.

True inner strength allows us to remain empathetic and maintain our flexibility. Like a palm tree surviving the storm with its roots firmly grounded, its trunk swaying cleverly, and its leaves flowing gracefully like feathers in the wind. This strength is what we strive for in our practice.

Lifting weights builds our outer strength, which will help us sail the oceans. Meditation builds our inner strength, which will help us sail through life.

Good morning, Sunday.
Let's meditate.

83

Seeing

My mind is still buzzing from the hurried activity on the city's streets, which preceded my visit to the museum. As I meander through the building, I enter a room filled with the presence of Cézanne, a master of still life. The setting in the room is soothing—soft lighting illuminates only where necessary, allowing the pieces to reveal themselves. I admire his artwork, and it propels me to examine the reflection and contemplation that went into each piece decorating the wall. One room opens up into another, and I continue to become absorbed in the life and mind of the artist.

How meticulously his pencil depicted what he saw and felt, applying shades of watercolor where needed and withholding brushstrokes to allow light and creativity to shine through. His profound observation was enhanced by his imagination, producing vibrant work that felt like it was moving even though it was still. I enter the final room with studies of landscapes and kitchen tables filled with glass bottles, ceramic vessels, and fresh fruit, my mind now wholly immersed. Multiple pieces of the same subject matter differ, as perception is ever-changing, even when we look at the same object many times.

As I leave the exhibition, I feel encouraged to be more attentive, to slow down and notice refinement in the details. To see like Cézanne is not only to look but to look again. We learn to see things in a different light, to elevate our vision and appreciate the experience of seeing.

Good morning, Sunday.
Let's meditate.

84

Motivation

There she comes again, it's Menopause, knocking on my front door. Every now and then, she comes to visit. I allowed her in once, and she wouldn't leave, like the undesirable guest who overstayed. My heart starts racing. "Please go away." She stands there patiently, hypnotizing me with her enticing eyes. She knocks again. This time she travels with friends: Anxiety and Overwhelm. They want to sit and have a cup of tea. Tears accumulate, and my eyes feel like heavy gray clouds waiting to explode. She remains calm and persistent. I notice that Doubt has come to join her team. I know that if I don't act now, they will realize that my door is unlocked. They will walk in and sit down. I will be stuck with them again, serving tea, cake, and cookies, with a fictitious smile.

I run upstairs searching for Motivation, my best friend who somehow quietly slipped away. I close my eyes, pause to connect with my breath. The answer always awaits, in the stillness of my being. I grab my sneakers and head out the back door. I go for a brisk

walk, a spin, a dance. I jump, I run, and I get my
blood flowing. My heart beats fast; this time, it feels
good. I feel the energy, life, running through me like
lightning. Motivation smiles as she squeezes my hand.
When I return, the visitors are gone. I am relieved and
happy. I can breathe again and get on with my day.

I know she'll be back; she left a note on the floor.
My sneakers will be ready, waiting at the door.

Good morning, Sunday.
Let's meditate.

85

Savasana

"Mix two cups of wholewheat flour with one cup of warm water in a medium bowl and knead it into a dough that is the perfect combination of soft, stiff, and pliable." I follow the instructions meticulously. Then I cover the bowl with a damp cloth and set it aside for thirty minutes. Now what? It's almost dinner time, and preparations have come to a complete halt while I stare at the dough as it proceeds to take its *savasana* with ease and comfort.* It is simply not practical, as it will delay my dinner schedule.

We have a similar attitude when considering rest. How can a nap in the middle of the day be productive? How can we stop what we are doing and pause? It seems inefficient and irresponsible.

---

* *Savasana* is a relaxing pose practiced at the end of a yoga practice, where the body is kept still in a supine position.

By removing opportunities to rest and connect with the breath throughout our day, we have become a society where we label continuous work as productive and consider resting as lazy. We have forgotten that the purpose of taking pauses, naps, or resting during our day is to recharge our body and mind. In this way, we can continue from a place of stillness and clarity rather than allowing ourselves to become exhausted and overwhelmed.

This week, I rediscovered the benefits of *savasana*. I have incorporated it into my day, allowing it to become my reset button. After twenty minutes of complete surrender to the breath and awareness, my mind and body feel restored and renewed.

The dough is now ready for the next step. I separate it into small portions, roll each one out with a rolling pin on a lightly floured surface, and put the first one on medium heat on the *tawa* (Asian frying pan). After I cook each side briefly, I roll it up and take the first bite. My chapati is perfect and divine, thanks to the *savasana*.

Good morning, Sunday.
Let's meditate.

86

Motherhood

Suddenly I got the part. I didn't even get a chance
to practice the lines. The casting director chose
me for one of the lead roles in this play called
Life, As We Know It. There I was, onstage, with
a handsome supporting actor by my side and
a village beside me. I had to figure out how
to raise these two children, a boy and a girl.
They were adorable and cuddly. The boy was
a natural conversationalist, and the girl was
talented beyond my imagination. I had to write
my lines and wing it. Right there, in front of the
live audience. It was an incredible experience.
Sometimes the little boy and girl would keep me
up all night, and on other occasions, they would
put my character to the ultimate test; I thought I
would throw my hands up and walk off the stage.
However, I stuck it out because, on the whole, it
was the most fulfilling, intriguing, and delightful
learning experience.

As the children grew, the role kept changing, and my character matured. First, I was the nurturer, and subsequently, my character evolved into a chef, teacher, project manager, organizer, nurse, counselor, chauffeur, chaperon, director of culture and entertainment, creative activity planner, mentor, emotional support leader, wise person, wiser person, and best friend. What an honor that the Creator selected me for the part. I will be forever grateful for being chosen and for the opportunity to serve in this role called "Mother."

Good morning, Sunday.
Let's meditate.

87

Recharging

Like our phones, we all need to recharge to gain back our energy and avoid burning out. Recharging is different from relaxing. We may relax by taking a nap or putting our feet up and sipping a glass of wine. Recharging involves resting the body and the mind so energy can rebuild itself from within, which takes time and is not something we can expedite. It requires patience. A great way to recharge is to step away from your usual daily routine and activities and get a change of scenery. Take a vacation or step out of your comfort zone and learn something new. Spend some time in nature, observing, breathing, or spend a day serving others and allow their expressions of gratitude to recharge you.

I have several ways of recharging. A good night's sleep is significant. Seven hours is my number. My body gets to rest and take a break from a long and exhausting day. Sometimes a brisk walk may be my recharge, as I may experience sluggishness after sitting at my desk for an extended time or if

I feel lethargic in the morning. My favorite recharge is a grounded yoga practice on my mat, followed by *savasana* and meditation. I get up feeling relaxed and ready to tackle the day with a calm and clear mind.

An essential part of recharging is to rest the mind. The mind does not rest when we walk, exercise, or even sleep. It may feel clear; however, it does not get a chance to shut down completely. It's like putting your car in park but never turning off the engine. One way to rest the mind is to slow down and focus on one thing. We can do this through the practice of meditation. I often hear people say that they can't meditate: It's challenging to sit still, or they feel agitated and restless. This is not unusual, as it is the nature of the mind to wander. The mind does not want to be still. It needs to be trained. Allow your mind to wander and explore the many different meditation methods until you find the one that works for you. The reward will be immeasurable.

Good morning, Sunday.
Let's meditate.

88

The Little Girl

A huge guango tree stands firmly in the villa's backyard. A vine wraps itself tightly around the trunk and climbs to the top, disappearing into the multitude of branches. I notice a bright yellow swing suspended from a large limb of the tree. It hangs there motionless, inviting me to have a seat in the present moment of stillness.

Eagerly, I accept the invitation. I sit down and hold on to the ropes on either side, ensuring that they are secure. I lift my heels off the ground playfully, allowing only the tips of my toes to connect to the earth. As I release my feet and surrender myself to the swing, I welcome the light sway. In a few minutes, my mind wanders to my childhood days, and the temptation to move grows stronger. I begin to sway to and fro like a pendulum moving through the air. I feel happy and carefree as the moderate movement takes me higher.

In a moment, the little girl in me tells me to go faster and faster. I oblige her wishes as I lean back and stretch my legs and toes out. "Higher," she says, "higher! Let's get someone to push us." "It's OK," I tell her, "I can do it all by myself!" I move swiftly, and I can now see the blue ocean up ahead as I swing forward, and I laugh as I feel as light as a bird gliding through the air.

After a while, I start to ease up; the girl jumps down and runs off to explore the garden on another adventure. The swing slows down and returns to stillness. I take a moment to embrace the pause and appreciate the gentle reminder that, inside me, that little girl who is fearless and carefree still exists when I am brave enough to let go and surrender.

Good morning, Sunday.
Let's meditate.

89

Words

Today I give gratitude to words.

Words give us the ability to communicate our thoughts and feelings. Choosing the right word to express what we mean is an art that takes precision and care. Selecting the appropriate word is like looking for a puzzle piece that has the perfect fit: We may see a piece that seems suitable; however, when trying it out, it is not exactly what we are looking for. When we find the correct piece, we experience that "aha moment."

When I write, the thesaurus is my best friend. I pick, choose, and refuse until I am satisfied with my selection. On other occasions, the correct word arises from a place of silence. As I find the perfect fit, I notice that often I can say what I mean in fewer words than I thought possible.

Sometimes, in our haste, we do not take the time to ponder word choice and resort to using excessive words to express ourselves. We lose our focus. Other times we choose words that may have a similar meaning but carry a different energy or intention. We hurt people's feelings. Being meticulous in our language encourages us to notice the power of words and be more accurate. The practice of word choice requires attention and discernment. In moments of stillness, the options become clear.

Good morning, Sunday.
Let's meditate.

90

A Lump Of Clay

It's Tuesday morning. I wake up early, finish my yoga practice, and head to my spin class. Getting a spot is like winning the lottery, as there are only ten bikes available. During the intense class, I wonder why I keep signing up to receive this torture. However, after sixty minutes, a sense of accomplishment explains my gratitude for hopping on.

My next stop is home, to shower and have a quick breakfast, and then I drive out to the country, where I will be taking my first pottery class. Being left-brain dominant, I have decided to step out of my comfort zone and try something different to stimulate the right side of my brain. Adding variety to my life once in a while keeps me balanced. It's like getting ahead on your paddleboard: You need to paddle left and right to move forward, or you will be going around in circles forever.

It's a one-hour drive to the studio. Once I am out of traffic, I listen to an inspirational podcast as I enjoy my drive in solitude. The studio lies on a large historical estate, hidden among tall trees and tropical foliage. It has thick, ancient stone walls, dusty floors, wooden benches, and wooden shelves stacked with carvings and beautiful handmade pieces.

Upon arrival, I feel embraced by nature's warmth and welcomed by birds chirping in the trees. Once I settle in, David, the teacher, explains some of the basics, and I realize that a notebook may have come in handy. I continue to listen attentively, hoping to retain all the information, but my mental notebook struggles to grasp every detail.

I conclude that the best way to learn is from experience. David hands me my first lump of clay. I roll out my clay with a rolling pin, ensuring I apply equal pressure on all sides, spinning the slab around as if I am preparing roti for dinner. Thankfully, as a result of this experience, I start to gain some confidence in my creation. Time does not seem to exist at the studio, as I become completely engrossed

in my work. While I knead the clay, it reminds
me of one of my favorite verses in the Chandogya
Upanishads:

> "As by knowing one lump of clay, dear one,
> We come to know all things made out of clay.
> That they differ only in name and form
> While the stuff of which all are made is clay." *

In this practical way, Uddalaka shares his wisdom by
explaining to his son Shvetaketu that all life is one.

After creating two pieces, I place them on the dusty
wooden shelf in the studio. A lump of clay has been
transformed into two coffee mugs. They differ only in
name and form; their essence is still clay.

Good morning, Sunday.
Let's meditate.

---

* *The Upanishads* (Chandogya Upanishads, translated by
Eknath Easwaren) vs. 6.1.4

91

Experience

I can tell you to sit behind the potter's wheel and
    steady yourself,
relax your shoulders and the tips of your toes.
Focus on being anchored
and use the heel of your hands to center your clay
    while the wheel spins rapidly.

I can tell you that the clay will move left and right,
trying to persuade your body to meet its demands.
You should remain stable, release apprehension,
and bring the clay back to center.

I can tell you to add water, be patient,
and allow my voice to guide your hands
as you maneuver the clay into the desired shape.
Be willing to let go of all expectations and breathe.

However,
it's only by sitting behind the wheel yourself
and experiencing the movement of the clay,
will you understand the art of pottery.

I can tell you to sit on your cushion and steady yourself,
relax your shoulders and the tips of your toes.
Focus on the eye center,
and use your breath to center your mind while your
    thoughts spin rapidly.

I can tell you that the thoughts will move from one
    thing to another,
trying to persuade the mind to meet its demands.
You should remain stable, release the thoughts,
and bring the mind back to center.

I can tell you to add a mantra,
be patient, and allow my voice to guide your thoughts
as you maneuver the mind to become one-pointed.
Be willing to let go of all expectations and breathe.

However,
it's only by sitting on your cushion with your Self
and experiencing the movement of the mind,
will you understand the true benefits of meditation.

Good morning, Sunday.
Let's meditate.

92

Intend And Allow

It's Tuesday morning. My spin class instructor has us riding on what appears to be Mt. Neverest. If my spin bike wasn't stationary, I could probably reach the studio on the hill in time for my pottery class at 10 a.m. However, by the time I arrive, I may feel like a lump of clay. After breakfast, I get in my Kia and tune into a playlist by the Piano Tribute Players. It reminds me of the rich, mellow harmony playing in the background as you board American Airlines. My children refer to it as elevator music; however, to me, it's a flashback to my traveling days.

It's a rainy day and muddy around the studio. Overcast skies cause the air to remain cool and damp. Today I will learn how to glaze the two coffee mugs I created last week. The glazing area is at the back of the studio behind the five kilns, a pile of logs, and a collection of glazed pieces waiting to be fired. There are large buckets on the floor filled with different glazes and smaller containers on a large wooden table. The studio cat, Luna, meanders

through the buckets exploring the area while her
kittens are tucked away safely in a large clay pot on
a shelf in an obscure corner of the studio.

After David explains the glazing technique, I sand
off and dust my pieces to ensure they are smooth
and clean while considering the glaze I wish to use.
What you see is not what you get, as the actual color
reveals itself in the kiln's heat. Therefore, it is best
to stick to the mantra, "Intend and allow," to set
my intention on what I wish my piece to look like,
and allow the kiln to unfold its beauty.

I take my time to apply the glaze meticulously,
using several layers to ensure I cover every spot
thoroughly. In my mind, I have an image of the
final product. I am mindful that my expectations
are not cast in stone, as this may result in
disappointment. Glazing is a practice of learning
to let go and accept results that are beyond
my control. I can resist by holding on, or I can
surrender to the element of surprise. I set my
intention by giving my full attention. Now it's in
the hands of Agni, the God of creative fire.

Good morning, Sunday.
Let's meditate.

93

Music

As the rays of the sun break the darkness, early morning tweets break the silence of the night. They start with one bird tweet while an owl hoots like a metronome in the background. Soon a whole orchestra participates, and the morning medley begins. Nature has its unique way of creating music. The birds' songs in the early morning are light-hearted, creating a cheerful feeling as the day commences.

After my morning routine, I break my silence by scrolling down to one of my New Age playlists and select one, which then echoes through our home. The first songs are Sanskrit hymns of gratitude and reverence, as I recognize every new day with appreciation. The choice of music changes as the day progresses.

As a lover of music, almost every genre has a space in my library. Some are more popular than others, so in return, they receive more ear time.

Music has the power to reconnect us with memories. Songs such as "I will survive" by Gloria Gaynor take me back to college days, dancing with my girlfriends in the dorm as we used the full capacity of our lungs.

Music also has the power to create a certain mood. When we arrive at the spa, we expect to hear soothing sounds, like ocean waves, rather than loud electric guitars in rock and roll. When I enter a space and am disenchanted by the music, my tolerance for remaining in this space is limited. On the other hand, when I am enjoying the music, I am in complete harmony, and time becomes timeless.

Whatever we experience through our senses affects our state of mind. The sounds that resonate with us will set the tone for our day as they have the power to reset our mind. Choose them with love.

Good morning, Sunday.
Let's meditate.

94

The Journey

I am on a journey to find my true nature.

Sometimes I stop to admire a flowing river or a field of flowers.

I may take a detour, lose my way, or even fall off the bike.

I never lose hope as I am determined and steadfast.

Along the way, I meet others who want me to follow them.

I enjoy the company and tag along, or get sidetracked by something that looks more attractive.

Eventually, the goal is to reach my destination and learn from the experiences I encounter on my quest.

It helps to use a map, so the mantra is my guide. It can show me the way, yet I still have choices: to go the fastest, shortest, or scenic route. This decision is mine to make.

Today I give gratitude for this journey, this opportunity to seek so I can find my true Self, in this lifetime or the next.

Good morning, Sunday.
Let's meditate.

95

Choice

I feel fortunate to live in a part of the world where I have the privilege of choice. However, this comes with responsibility. Some choices affect our lives, our environment, or the lives of others, as we are not the only inhabitants on this planet. Therefore, some choices we make require deeper contemplation.

Last week I spent a few days at the beach. One afternoon, I noticed a man walk out of the sea, holding two beautiful deep-orange starfish. The following day, while paddleboarding, I marveled at a bright starfish lying peacefully on a white sandy background in the shallow water. As I continued, I noticed families of starfish radiating in hues of orange beneath me on the ocean floor. It upset me that someone would choose to remove these echinoderms from their natural habitat and try to sell them on the beach.

Early the next morning, while he was swimming in the same area, a tiny jellyfish stung my husband on his arm. He captured it in a cup. We placed it on our breakfast table as a centerpiece and marveled that something small and beautiful to the eye could cause so much pain. We now had to decide what to do with "Jelly the fish." We certainly were not going to put it on our toast. I recalled the man walking with the starfish. Is a starfish more essential than a jellyfish?

After some thought, we called Raymond, the paddleboard pro. He balanced the cup on the front of his board, skillfully paddled way out toward the horizon, and safely returned the jellyfish to the ocean. Some decisions may seem trivial; however, each choice we make has relevance, especially when it involves other beings. Take a moment to pause.

Good morning, Sunday.
Let's meditate.

96

The Places
I Call Home

After working on the road for a week, there is
nothing more appealing than coming home.
Home has several meanings to me, but two hold
particular significance.

One is Curaçao, where I was born and raised.
When I land in the country where I took my
first steps, a feeling of comfort embraces me.
The moment I step off the airplane, the breeze
invigorates me like blood rushing through my
veins. My first thought is always: Welcome home.
I remember my parents and my childhood—the
time when I was cared for and watched over.
A sense of security and acceptance surrounds
me. No matter how long I've been away, the
familiarity of home will never lose its fragrance.

My second home is in Jamaica, the country where
I've lived for the last thirty-two years. Jamaica
has a different homely feeling for me.

It represents being independent, raising a family, making new friends, and creating memories. It's where I matured into the person I am today and learned to choose a fulfilling and meaningful life. It's where I cultivated a sense of belonging by embracing the island I now call home.

What are the qualifications for a place to be called "home?" For me, it is that place that resonates with all my senses, where my eyes see familiar faces and places. My taste buds are satisfied by comfort food: chicken and rice with callaloo, or "sate ku batata"—always my first meal after being away. Home is where music and language sound like a song I can sing because I know all the words. I smell the fresh salty air of the ocean breeze while my toes wiggle as they touch the sand, and feel the love of family and friends. Home is the blanket of contentment that I can snuggle up in and rest.

Home is where the heart is. I only have one heart, but I have two homes, and they are both as sweet as can be.

Good morning, Sunday.
Let's meditate.

97

Silence

How do I feel when silence surrounds me?

Do I feel afraid, insecure, bored, or alone?
Do I need to call a friend, grab my phone, get a glass of
  wine, or a cup of coffee?
Or do I feel serene?

What am I connecting to?
Should I invite some noise in to drown out the silence?
I could turn on some music, maybe the TV?

Or should I just stay at ease?

Below all these layers within myself is a place of peace,
  a moment of stillness.
If I can just dig beneath all the layers, somehow peel
  them away,
I know I can find it.
I know I can escape the noise within my head,
  the chitter and chatter, the fear, doubt, and panic.
So I practice every day.
I sit every day.
Until one day,
when the silence within me recognizes the silence that
  surrounds me
I feel at peace with myself and the world.

Good morning, Sunday.
Let's meditate.

98

Coffee Breaks

There's a French cafe in the departure lounge of JFK airport. Whenever I pass through, I stop and have a cappuccino and a croissant. A lovely petite lady works there. She's always by herself.

It's 8 a.m. on a Monday, and the terminal is bustling as many flights are departing at this time of the day. Travelers are rushing about trying to grab a quick breakfast and a snack to carry on the plane. The lady in the French cafe has a full house and is entirely focused on her tasks. She has to welcome and seat all her customers, take their orders, and enter them into the computer that sends the order to the kitchen. She clears and sets the tables, wipes down the bar, puts the dishes in the dishwasher, makes fresh espresso and cappuccino, serves beverages, brings the customers their food and the check, and collects payments.

I take a seat at the bar, place my order, and watch her as she moves about continuously, utterly focused on her work. She is swift and efficient, precise, and polite in her speech, and makes eye contact with all her customers. She glides around the cafe like a bee buzzing from one flower to the next. While she executes her chores, every movement is precise and well thought out, so that she makes use of every moment as she follows her master plan.

She notices that I place my money on the counter. As she clears the table next to me, she takes my payment and brings me my check. For a moment, I am confused. I remind her that she hasn't brought me my coffee yet. She looks at me and says that she is aware and politely asks for me to be patient as she is by herself. I apologize and reprimand myself quietly for being insensitive. After all, she did look like she knew exactly what she was doing.

She makes a fresh cappuccino and places it in front of me. I thank her and continue to watch her as I sip my drink. I wonder how she manages day in, day out to do this by herself, and I admire her for being so capable. I wonder if she gets a moment to pause and sip a cup of coffee after the morning rush.

We all get caught up in our daily chores and routines. C'est la vie. Some days are easier than others. Today is one of my easy days. I get to sit at a French cafe and watch someone else whizz through their to-do list. I think about tomorrow when I will be at my desk in the office in a similar frame of mind, checking off item by item. Will I go nonstop and skip lunch? Will I take a moment to sip a cup of tea? When we are in the midst of our day, it's easy to get caught up in the wave of action. We don't realize until the wave washes us up on the shore and spits us out, completely depleted.

I am tempted to offer the lady my cappuccino but imagine that she would think it's absurd. Instead, I leave her a cash tip and leave myself a mental tip: I will approach my desk tomorrow one step at a time, remembering to stop and take a moment to sip water before continuing with the next task. I realize that it seems like we are getting a lot done when we flow from one thing to the next; it could almost look like a performance at the theater. However, even at the theater, the actors need to go backstage to change, and we all look forward to a short intermission to get some popcorn!

Good morning, Sunday.
Let's meditate.

99

The Present Moment

Today I give gratitude to the present moment.

At the crack of dawn, my eyes open. A dim light attempts to sneak in through the cracks in the tightly shut wooden louvers. I get up and open the door to my verandah that faces the ocean. The sky boasts hints of light orange as the sun awakens, promising another hot and sunny day. I step onto the sand and walk to the far east corner of the beach, where I spread my blanket under a thatched beach umbrella to start my practice. After a few minutes, I hear drops of rain splattering. Gradually the drizzle escalates into pouring rain, and I am trapped under my umbrella, immersed in the surround sound of an orchestra of water. The rain fluctuates from a soft patter to a deafening clatter, with crashing waves participating as cymbals.

My mind goes into planning mode, deciding whether I should stay or move. Will I get wet?

How long will this last? Dozens of questions start popping into my head. Finally, I decide to listen and enjoy the music provided by nature in the present moment. There is nowhere to go. A few minutes ago, I was convinced that the day would be sunny; however, nature had a different plan.

Over the last few months, being present has become a familiar practice. We don't know what to expect from one day to the next, or even from one moment to the next. I am learning to slow down, be present, and appreciate the day for what it has to offer. Although the weather may seem bleak now, there is always something to be grateful for. Find it.

Good morning, Sunday.
Let's meditate.

100

Simplicity

My frequent flyer status was interrupted, accompanied by a drastic change in lifestyle. However, last week I was able to escape, and this morning I checked in for my flight to head back home. After the lengthy check-in procedure, I went to my usual spot at Miami International Airport, got myself a cortadito with a pandebono, sat down, and enjoyed the moment.

How often have I done this in the past and taken this snack for granted? I was too busy thinking about everything except what was right in front of me. Over the years, travel has become a lot more complicated, yet we still make an effort to fly. We go through a tremendous amount of inconvenience to experience a change in scenery. In our longing to fulfill our desires, we forget how divine that one cup of coffee is just before we board our flight. Today, I give gratitude to those moments of simplicity throughout our lives that we so often overlook. What else are we taking for granted?

Here's to the best cup of coffee for US$1.50 and a warm piece of bread that has the flavor of cheese.

Good morning, Sunday.
Let's meditate.

Alone

ALOne

ALLOne

ALLone

ALL one

101

All One

As the holidays approach,
and
we remember those
who we have lost,
do not feel alone;
pause and notice,
we are all united,
we are never alone,
because
we are all one.

Good morning, Sunday.
Let's meditate.

102

Letters

I grew up in a time when we wrote letters to
communicate with our friends and relatives who were
overseas. Much thought went into reading, writing, and
the presentation of a letter. For me, it was a meticulous
affair. In summer, we would travel to England to
visit my uncle. I would buy beautiful stationery with
matching envelopes from WHSmith, a popular stationery
store. Some had borders of overlapping bright yellow
sunflowers with a checkered copper-brown trim. Others
were crisp white paper with Snoopy sitting on the red
roof of his doghouse, typing away diligently on his
manual typewriter.

Our parents weren't as particular about their stationery.
They used a pale blue, ultra-thin, foldable all-in-one
mailer. Once sealed, it had a slim blue-and-red striped
border with "Air mail" marked on the front. Perfect for
making paper airplanes, as it already had the trim that
resembled the American Airlines logo all around it. They
said it would get there faster, as if it could fly by itself.

I would choose the most suitable stationery, based on
who I was writing to. Once I mailed the letter, I would
wait in suspense for the reply, which could take up to

two months, depending on the speed of the mail and the response time of the recipient. I kept in touch, building friendships and reconnecting with loved ones, in this way. Birthdays were delightful, as I received cards that I displayed in my room. Each one I read carefully and preserved for years in a dedicated letter box.

Later, when I was in college, the mailroom was the most exciting or depressing place to be, depending on whose mailbox was next to yours. My eyes would widen, and my heart would race when I peeked into the tiny window of my mailbox, which revealed the long-awaited letter. I analyzed the handwriting and tried to guess who it was from before turning it around to see the return address. Then came the decision whether to rip it open or carefully open it to preserve the beautiful stationery. I read with attention and kept it close by so I could reread it before saving it in my letter box. Letters were more precious than phone calls. They allowed you to hold on to a little piece of the person who wrote them and preserve their message until you were ready to let go.

Today, email, messaging, and social media have completely changed our way of communicating. In addition to speeding things up, they also allow us to keep in touch with many more friends and relatives, make new friends, and rediscover old ones. We can send birthday wishes, letters, notes, and jokes, and share pictures at a click of a button. We are living in a world of quantity. Although I appreciate the convenience, and the opportunity to reach out to many, I still love to receive cards on special occasions. My family knows that at Christmastime, the card is an essential gift under the tree. Much thought goes into getting the perfect card for someone. It's never a random choice, and usually something humorous, with enough space to write a personal message. Before we open our gifts, we open our cards and share our thoughts and feelings, which are more precious than anything else.

When is the last time you wrote a letter or a handwritten note? Imagine the joy you could bring to someone's day.

Good morning, Sunday.
Let's meditate.

103

Commitment To A Gratitude Practice

I woke up at 4 a.m. feeling anxious about all the things on my to-do list. I tossed and turned and finally got up and started writing. I committed to doing a twenty-five-day gratitude practice, hoping it would keep me calm and grounded. I completed this on Christmas Day, after which it developed into a weekly Sunday gratitude message to reflect on.

Focusing on things to be grateful for has shifted my awareness to creating an appreciation for the little things in life, rather than focusing on imperfections, problems, and never-ending to-do lists. I am gradually learning to pause, enjoy, and appreciate my things to do, one at a time, rather than rushing to get them all done. Along the way, I have come across many details I used to take for granted or ignore. The intention of this life is not to let them go unnoticed but to look for the beauty in the details and allow them to enrich our lives. They are like the elements of fine wine or the final touches on an artist's masterpiece.

Whatever the practice is, consistency is vital. When we adhere to our commitment, we will notice a change. I can only share my experience and trust in the reward that comes with consistency. I still panic at times; by no means have I become Ms. Grateful—calm, cool, and collected. However, when I pause to reflect on gratitude, the painting changes right before my eyes, and life doesn't seem so overwhelming.

Good morning, Sunday.
Let's meditate.

104

Birds

I sit under the tree in my backyard every morning to do my meditation practice. A few birds live in this tree. I notice that the same bird wakes up at minutes to seven every morning. She is consistent with her timing. She starts chirping in a particular way, and a crescendo of morning tweets follows.

Soon after this, the birds' lives are in full swing. In the spring, one of them was making its nest. As I sat in stillness, she flew by and grazed the top of my head, creating a rush of wind. Maybe she felt threatened by my presence and thought I was there to harm her. She did this for a few mornings. I sat unruffled, breathing in and out, and continued with my practice. She realized that I was just a peaceful observer. Now, I am part of her habitat, and she no longer fears my presence.

This morning the activity in the tree seems busier than usual. I hear many varying tweets and chirps. There is a lot of excitement going on, and many more birds are present. Perhaps they are preparing for Christmas as they may have a full house. It could be that they are aware of my children coming home for the holidays, and it's a reflection of my excitement. Or maybe word got out about the rental market, and they started an Airbnb for the birds and bees in this tree for the winter season!

Whatever the reason is, I love waking up every morning to their cheerful spirit—hearing the chipper melody in the background, preparing a breakfast of positivity. What a perfect way to
start my ho-ho-ho-holiday.

Good morning, Sunday.
Let's meditate.

105

The Guest Room

My mother was one of many, and so, when we were growing up, we traveled across the globe to visit her siblings in England, Spain, and the Philippines. Travel was a privilege. We dressed up in our finest clothes and went to the airport to start our journey. My mother wore her printed pantsuit, carried a gift for our host and her box-shaped vanity case, which contained every cream, lotion, and perfume she owned. I wore a polka-dot dress and my black patent leather shoes. When we arrived, we stayed in the guest room. My mother unpacked all our clothes and put them away neatly. She made her bed when she woke up and kept the room immaculate. She taught us to respect the space of our host.

The guest room is a sacred space. It does not have an owner and sees many faces. Its walls hold secrets, which they never reveal to other visitors. It is nonjudgmental and welcomes everyone with the same grace and ease, no matter their differences.

Over the years, I have had the privilege of staying in many guest rooms and enjoyed my visits as if I was at home. I had friends and family around me and a comfortable place to rest and have a meal. As a host, it's an honor to have visitors in our guest room. They fill our home with life and love, and we take care of them with enthusiasm and pleasure. One of the ancient Hindu scriptures, the Taittiriya Upanishads, describes this as "Atithi Devo Bhava": Be one for whom the guest is God.[*] As Christmas approaches, this is an ideal reminder to spruce up our guest room and set our table with an extra plate. You never know who may show up for dinner, or whose sleigh may break down on our rooftop!

Good morning, Sunday.
Let's meditate.

---

* Eshwar Bhakti, "Meaning of Atithi Devo Bhava" (no date), https://pujayagna.com/blogs/hindu-customs/atithi-devo-bhava, accessed August 2023

106

Sparkle

I walk into my living room, and the glistening of the water in the distance draws my attention. I stop, sit down, and take a few minutes to admire this moment. My eyes close, and I feel the Christmas breeze caressing my face. It's cool and crisp, suggesting that a fresh start is on the horizon when a new day begins. How easy it is to allow these moments of gratitude to slip away from us. How uplifting it is when we take the time to notice the miracles that lie right before our eyes. The end of the year can be tumultuous as we fall into the trap of taking on more than our mind can digest, causing us to become overwhelmed.

These snippets during the day are what give me strength. They are reminders that even though life can become hectic, there is always an opportunity to notice a sparkle. The evening comes quickly, and I am exhausted. I manage to cross a few items off my list and add one or two more when I sharpen my memory. My lunch becomes dinner, and I sit down with a glass of wine on our chestnut-colored sofa. An aroma of pine fills the room, inviting me to close my eyes and take in the scent of nature as holiday tunes play softly in the background. I admire the shimmer in the tree as it stands there peacefully in the corner, reminding me of the opportunity to notice the sparkle.

Good morning, Sunday.
Let's meditate.

107

The Backstage Crew

There are those who live their lives backstage. They are the type of people who choose not to be in the limelight. They love the inconspicuous job that requires attention but does not draw attention. Sometimes they appear onstage to take a peek and experience the action. However, they swiftly get pushed aside by envy and egos that thrive in the spotlight, reminding them to settle back into the shade, where they cannot steal the show.

Yet the background of a painting enhances the image, and the background music at an event sets the mood. Its strength and beauty are in its subtleness. The person in the background is where the work begins and ends. They are the fertilizer in the garden or the street sweeper who appears after sunset. They are the person we depend on to show up so that we can perform onstage. Without them, we are simply a nomination.

Today I give gratitude to the backstage crew.
The one who puts on the coffee in the morning,
the one who washes the dishes for us to use,
the one who prices the merchandise or stocks the shelf,
the one who takes notes and sends reminders,
the one who wipes the floors after the event,
the one who turns off the lights.
The person with no hashtags
who is never seen and occasionally heard,
without whose presence the event would have been absent.

Good morning, Sunday.
Let's meditate.

108

108 Drops

Drip, drip, drip, the bucket fills.

There's a pipe in my backyard that keeps on dripping. At first, I ignored it—until the water bill arrived. There are days when the practice is challenging and the mind continues to wander about. Then I glimpse a promise of stillness, and the mind settles in.

108 drops in my bucket. 108 messages of gratitude. 108 mornings that we have sat together in meditation.

Every moment of gratitude fills my heart. Every meditation is a step toward a kind, clear, and calm mind. Stay committed, stay focused, every drop counts.

Good morning, Sunday.
Let's meditate.

Building A Practice

Wherever I am in the world, I start my day with meditation. If you would like to start a meditation practice, I suggest finding a teacher who can guide you as there are many different types of meditation. Finding one that works for you is a journey.

Here are some simple steps you can follow to get the most out of your meditation experience:

- Choose a time and try to practice at the same time every day.

- Pick a spot somewhere quiet, peaceful, and away from distractions—somewhere that you can sit every day, not your bed. Make it your own.

- Have a comfortable seated position. With the spine straight, and feet on the floor, sit on a chair or on the floor, using blankets or cushions to make yourself stable and comfortable.

- You may start with a routine (this is not necessary; however, it may be helpful). An example could be:

  » Some simple stretches to ease your sitting posture

  » A breathing exercise to center the mind

  » Reading something inspiring or uplifting

- Start with one minute a day and work up to three minutes and then five. You can do anything for one minute. Set a realistic time limit that is achievable. Start small, and then watch your practice grow.

Before you know it, you will be sitting for fifteen minutes. After three weeks, it will become a habit. After six weeks, it will be part of your daily routine.

- Have no expectations. Sometimes the mind is active and sometimes it settles easier; the goal is not to have a goal.

- Be kind to yourself. Meditation isn't about right or wrong. It's about allowing you to find your true nature.

- If your mind wanders, gently shift it back to your mantra.

- Avoid being judgmental about yourself and your practice. Enjoy your practice, and you will look forward to your daily meditation.

There are different meditation techniques. If you are new to meditation and are considering starting a meditation practice, So'ham is a lovely place to start. You can find information on the So'ham meditation practice at www.himalayaninstitute.org.

The Awareness Exercise

It can be beneficial during the day to take a moment to pause and be present. I call it pressing the pause or refresh button. The Awareness Exercise is a method taught at The School of Practical Philosophy and Meditation that helps you to return to the present moment. You can find more information about the school on their website: www.philosophyworks.org.

If you want transformation, make a daily reservation with your meditation.

Acknowledgments

This book would never have become a reality without the encouragement of my friends and social media readers, who often suggested writing a book to me. I would laugh and say: "What will I write about?" Then I started writing.

I am grateful for all who believed in my writing skills before I believed in them myself. Thank you for reading my letters, reflections, and stories and continuing to ask me to write a book.

Thank you to Denny, for always being supportive on my journey to self-discovery and for being patient while I worked for hours on my manuscript; to Praveen, for gifting me my first online writing class and inspiring me to write; to Minali, for your encouragement and advice on design and execution.

To my friend and author Jessica Huie, whom I coincidentally met for the first time in a Pilates class recently, for a purpose, this would have never happened without you. There are no coincidences.

To my friend and talented artist Susan Clare, whose work I love and admire, thank you for accommodating me and delivering the illustrations and a beautiful cover on such short notice.

Thank you to my lovely photographer, Nomi Ellenson May, who, with a click of her finger, reveals the beauty in everything and everyone.

I am thankful to my teachers at the Himalayan Institute,
who have inspired and guided me in building the
foundation of my practice.

To my tutors and family at the School of Practical
Philosophy and Meditation for supporting my meditation
practice and for good company.

To the editors and staff at Rethink Publishing, Kathleen,
Anke, Jack, Joe, and Jennifer; as a first-time author, I
had many questions and appreciated the time you took
to answer them. It has been a pleasure working with you
and a positive learning experience.

The Author

In 2018 Veena began sharing her daily reflections online. After twenty-five days she stopped, only to be contacted by multiple friends asking why she had paused. Discovering that people were reading and gaining a sense of calm and presence through her reflections, the seed of an idea for a book was sown.

Journaling and meditation have supported Veena throughout her life and led to her completing her 500-hour yoga teacher training at the Himalayan Institute in Honesdale, Pennsylvania.

Today she continues to be a student at the School of Practical Philosophy and Meditation in NY.

A mother and grandmother, Veena loves children and frequently visits the SOS Children's Village in Montego Bay to spend time with the children and give them the love and attention they need.

Equally, Spandana Society in Hyderabad, India, is a place where Veena and her husband have sponsored children's education for many years.

Veena's parents left India in the 1950s and settled in Curaçao, a Dutch island in the Caribbean, where she was born, raised, and lived until she was twenty-one.

Having lived with her husband in the Virgin Islands for several years, they are now settled in Jamaica, where she presently works as a manager in retail.

***

Royalties from the sale of this book will go to SOS Children's Villages, Montego Bay, Jamaica, and Spandana Society in Hyderabad, India.

SOS Children's Villages, Jamaica, is a private, nongovernmental social development organization founded in 1970, which works with children who have lost parental care under a rights-based approach as defined by the International Convention of the Rights of the Child and the Child Care and Protection Act of Jamaica. Learn more at: www.sos-jamaica.org/who-we-are.

Spandana Society is an NGO that shelters, educates, and cares for former orphans and disadvantaged youth in Hyderabad, India. Learn more at: www.spandanasociety.in.

Children are our future. Invest in them by giving them the opportunity to be educated, and teaching them to be kind, compassionate, independent, and responsible.

224

www.ingramcontent.com/pod-product-compliance
Lightning Source LLC
Chambersburg PA
CBHW011159090426
42740CB00020B/3404